PRINCESSES & PORNSTARS

Emily Maguire is the author of the novels *The Gospel According to Luke* and *Taming the Beast*. Her articles and essays on sex, religion, culture and literature have been widely published, including in the *Sydney Morning Herald*, the *Griffith Review*, the *Observer* and the *Age*.

To Hilary and Matilda,

PRINCESSES & PORNSTARS

SEX • POWER • IDENTITY

EMILY MAGUIRE

Lovely to meet you
& all the best to
Matilda.

E Maguire.

Text Publishing Melbourne Australia

The Text Publishing Company
Swann House
22 William Street
Melbourne Victoria 3000
Australia
www.textpublishing.com.au

This edition published 2008

Design by Chong
Typeset by J & M Typesetting
Printed and bound by Griffin Press

National Library of Australia
Cataloguing-in-Publication data:

Maguire, Emily, 1976-
Princesses and pornstars : sex, power, identity / author, Emily Maguire.
Melbourne : Text Publishing Company, 2008.
9781921351310 (pbk.)

Women--Social conditions.
Women in popular culture. Women--Identity.
Feminism. Conservatism. Sex discrimination against women.
305.42

For Madeline

Contents

Introduction: Sex Power Identity

A typical woman

I am not someone you would describe as butch or femme, mannish or girly. I could not reasonably be considered 'one of the girls' nor am I part of any boys' club. In fact, I don't identify with or aspire to belong to any group, gendered or otherwise. If you asked me who I am I would say I'm a writer and I would find it hard to go further than that.

But here's the thing, I keep being confronted by the realisation that I am A Woman. I've used initial caps so you know I don't mean I'm confronted by the fact that I am female. Being female doesn't confront or bother me; my sex is just part of the fabric of which I am made. What bothers me is that the world expects me to behave and respond in ways that conform to an idea of A Woman that have nothing to do with who I am.

Growing up, I was told that girls could do anything boys could—that men and women were equal in every way. I believed this. More than believed, I *felt* it. I knew I was not defined by my gender, that the things I thought and did were expressions of my 'Emily-ness', not my femaleness. But by the time I reached my teens, I came to realise that other people would view me as female first and a person second, regardless of how I saw myself, and would project onto me their idea of what 'girl' or 'woman' meant. So it is that I have spent fifteen years failing to meet expectations I never set up: to value my appearance over my intellect; to be demure about sexuality; to defer to others (especially male others); to be a mother and homemaker.

There's a widespread belief that the sexual revolution and the women's rights movement of the 1960s and 1970s freed women from the tired old Virgin/Whore and Spinster Aunt/Glowing Housewife archetypes into which we used to be placed according to our sexual behaviour and marital status. If only this were true. While the professional and legal position of women has improved enormously in the last half-century, socially and domestically we've barely progressed at all. We are still judged first on how well we conform to gendered norms that were already looking tattered in 1955.

Back then, the value of a woman was determined by her sexual behaviour, function and fecundity. As it was, so it remains. In the apparently 'post-feminist' twenty-first century we still give air time to religious fundamentalists panicking about the sexual 'purity' of girls and women. Meanwhile, social and political conservatives are increasingly interested in the occupancy rate of our wombs. The lad-mag boofheads and slick city strip-club patrons are mostly concerned with the secondary sexual characteristics—tits and arse—while the women's glossy crowd is obsessed with how women's mouths, hands and vaginas can be used to orgasmify the worthy men of the world.

The news media churn out moral panic stories about girls dressing like prostitutes, talking dirty on the internet or giving boys blow-jobs in the back of the classroom, or run lasciviously illustrated features about the uptake of pole-dancing classes and female-run strip clubs. When there are no slutty schoolgirl or sexy lady stories to run, we get reports on the rising abstinence and modesty movements that train young people to deny their sexuality altogether.

Meanwhile, television programs such as 'Australian Princess' and 'The Bachelor', with their Cinderella story lines, attract thousands of would-be contestants and hundreds of thousands of viewers. In the real world, marriage is experiencing a peak in popularity amongst young people, and motherhood is all the rage. And rather than working at how to balance babies and careers, more and more young women are 'opting-out' (a loaded term if there ever was one) of the workforce and 'embracing' the full-time housewife roles their mothers and grandmothers struggled to escape.

Even the Saturday morning music video shows, which appear to be exemplars of raunch culture, are pushing gender roles circa 1950: women compete against each other for the affections of men; physical appearance is a woman's most valuable asset; sex is useful to get what you want, but don't enjoy it or you're a 'ho'; the most desirable man is the one who spends lots of money on 'his girl'.

While I guess we shouldn't expect anything different from pop culture, religious fundamentalists and meddling conservatives, it's disturbing to find the bipolar model is the dominant one in writing by, about and for women. The models of sexuality present in recent critiques of popular culture are almost always either 'girls gone wild' or 'chaste virgins looking for true love'. Some analyses make the former look fun and the latter prudish; others call the former tragic and the latter wise. Either way, there is little current analysis of actual female desire and behaviour.

Young women are *told* they can be and do anything, yet in the eyes of the media and mainstream culture the choices are still either/or. You can be a mother or have a proper career. You can have orgasms or respect. You can be independent or adored.

How women (never men) become empowered

Despite all this, we continually hear that feminism is a thing of the past. Even many who revere feminism as a movement do so in the past tense. It was an important and necessary movement, they say. Those feminists changed the world and for that I am thankful, they say. They were so successful, they say, that the movement is now unnecessary. The feminists won. Equality is ours.

And I wish they were right. I would love to wake up tomorrow and find that my gender has become all but irrelevant. I would love to go even one day without seeing articles about out-of-control girls (but never boys), classified ads for sex-lines staffed by women (never men) and commercials pitching laundry powder, nappies and shower cleaner to Mums (never Dads). I dream of walking past my local park and seeing as many men as women playing with their kids and of opening the business or sports section of the newspaper and seeing as many female names as male. And while it's beyond utopian for me to imagine well-meaning acquaintances might stop asking me when I'm going to have a baby, it would be nice if my husband could field the question some of the time.

Yes, it would be fantastic if feminism had been so successful that it was no longer necessary. But we need it just as much as we ever did and it's worrying that so many people refuse to acknowledge this. Instead, they use bizarrely circular logic to argue that, since feminism was about giving women choice and feminism succeeded, every choice a woman makes now is proof of feminism's success.

This reasoning is behind the maddening habit of labelling everything a woman does as 'empowering'. Stripping is empowering, so is being a stay-at-home mother. Watching porn is empowering, and so is withholding one's virginity until the right man comes along. A girl is empowered by new shoes and Brazilian waxes, and by handing over the family finances to her husband. Women, if the mainstream media are to be believed, are becoming more powerful with every wax-strip, lap-dance, oven-scrub and baby-bath.

And my question is, if all of this is so empowering, why the hell aren't men doing it? How come men manage to control the political, legal and business worlds without having first been empowered by taking off their clothes for magazines, pole-dancing or submitting to spousal authority? The issue is not whether a woman might *want* to do these things—it's none of anyone's business what an adult does with her life—but let's not kid ourselves that every choice a woman makes gives her power. Let's stop pretending that we no longer need feminism because we have the right to wear a glittery G-string while breast-feeding a baby and shopping for shoes.

One idea that often goes hand-in-hand with this 'empowering' nonsense, as a reason feminism is not needed, is that 'women already rule the world'. This is usually uttered by a hapless husband whose wife has just pouted her way into a new pair of diamond earrings. People who declare that women rule the world remind me of parents who say their toddler rules their household. They're talking about helpless creatures who get what they need by being cute and—when that doesn't work—throwing tantrums. It's what marketers call 'pester power' and it's what men are talking about when they chuckle and tell you their cute girlfriend sulked until she got that new kitchen. Toddlers and women who have no economic, political or social power don't rule a thing, no matter how many headaches they give their parents/men.

This false equation between nag power and social and political power contributes to what I call unidentified feminism. This is where a person (almost always a man) will complain that women have it easier than men because they control access to sex, are able to quit work when they have kids, don't have to take the garbage out or change car tyres or kill spiders or die in horrible wars or anything else that men must do while women get a free pass. To those who utter the above complaints I say: welcome to the feminist movement. Ending gendered expectations and privileges is what we're all about.

I need to be clear here that I am not a spokesperson for the feminist movement; to the best of my knowledge no such person exists and that is as it should be. Feminism is the broadest of churches and, just as there are plenty of feminists with whom I disagree, there will be plenty who disagree with me. How else could it be in a movement born of dissent and fuelled by discussion and debate? But, given the many feminisms out there, I want to define mine so I can continue to use the word as a shortcut for what I *do* mean rather than all the things I don't.

My feminism is based on the belief that, while there are differences between men and women, none of them justifies one sex having more social, economic or political power than the other. When I talk about feminist objectives I'm talking about destroying all sex and gender-based power differences in our society.

Apart from the obvious physical stuff, the differences between men and women are determined by cultural training. There is nothing inherently female about the desire to wear make-up and high heels, the ability to change nappies and wash dishes or the preference for wine over beer. There is nothing gendered about wanting to have a fulfilling career or to be a nurturing parent. There is no biological imperative to watch soppy movies or football, to admire pretty clothes or shiny cars. We all know this, I think, but we continue to fall back on these lazy excuses to explain why men do x and women do y because it's easier than the alternative, which is to think of each other simultaneously as individuals each with his or her own set of preferences and desires *and* as products and reinforcers of a culture.

There's another big objection to feminism these days and it's based on the idea that the problems facing girls and women in our society are caused by crazy women like me who want to destroy gender-based power differentials. This line of thought says that what I (and many others) see as women going backwards in society is just a return to the inevitable way of things after the brief aberration of female liberation. Women really are, like Eve, irresponsible, amoral flesh-bags filled with hormones, and if those hormones are not kept in control by the structures of a traditional family then the flesh-bags will go nuts and start humping everything in sight.

Or, more politely, that women who conform to conservative gender roles are happy, healthy, wealthy and wise because they are living the way nature intended. As evidence, we're told to look to the misery of young starlets who begin by flashing their lady-parts at the paparazzi and end up with a shaved head and a hellish crack addiction, or to the middle-aged women who were sexually promiscuous and professionally focused in their youth and are now lonely, husbandless and forever barren.

I ask those who think this way to consider that perhaps the problem is not with the nature of women but with something external to them. I ask you to consider the possibility that the problem is not with women being scatty or slutty or greedy or lazy or wanting it all or not knowing what they want, but is instead with the narrow way women are perceived and the way these narrow perceptions create a social, economic and political environment in which women are punished for not conforming.

Why the feminist police couldn't care less about your grooming habits

Something that turns a lot of women off feminism is the idea that it is prescriptive and judgmental, that if you don't live a feminist-approved lifestyle you'll have your feminist membership card torn up by the feminist police. This is nonsense. First, feminism isn't a club; there's no admission process, no executive committee and no rules. Second, feminism isn't a lifestyle; it's not about wearing the right outfit, having the right job and spouting out the right lines at dinner parties. Conversely, it's not something that wearing a push-up bra or becoming a full-time mother or admitting to a love of *Vogue* magazine will disqualify you from.

I'm not arguing that any choice is a feminist choice, but that feminists are human. Which means we sometimes make poor decisions and we sometimes contradict ourselves, and we sometimes do the best we can to live up to our ideals in a world that is very, very far from feminist-friendly. This is why none of us should judge other women for the choices they make or feel guilty for our own choices. Women cope with enough of that crap without feminists adding to it out of misguided ideological zeal.

So it might seem paradoxical that I spend a lot of time in this book discussing personal lives and choices. Back in the 1960s when the modern feminist movement was taking flight, many activists thought that women's 'personal problems' were just that—personal—and had no relevance to what was a political movement to obtain equal pay and legal rights for women. Housework, childcare, sex and body image were all matters of private choice and conscience to be figured out by individual women and their partners.

In 1969 the American activist Carol Hanisch wrote a memo to her colleagues in the women's liberation movement arguing against this way of thinking. Hanisch's memo became an essay and the title of that essay, 'The Personal is Political', became the catchcry for a movement. This phrase is referring to the fact that political forces influence—sometimes rule—our personal lives. It does not mean, as some have since claimed, that everything a woman does is a political statement. And it was never meant to be used, as it often is, to justify any action a woman takes as feminist or, conversely, to condemn anything that upsets a woman as sexist. Understanding that the personal is political means acknowledging that many 'personal problems' are created or exacerbated by political and social structures.

It's in the interests of oppressors to convince the underclass that they are not a class at all, but a set of individuals each with his or her own problems that he or she must solve for him or herself. Many women are told that their struggles with balancing work, children and relationships, and their battles with body image and sexuality, are problems they have to negotiate and juggle and solve.

The 1960s feminists organised consciousness-raising groups in order to address this issue. They gathered women together to talk about the common problems they faced in their lives and pointed out that in many cases the causes were systemic and political. Women who experienced unwanted pregnancy, rape, domestic violence, workplace discrimination and stifling domestic lives learnt that their personal problems were shared by women from all kinds of backgrounds. Through feminist consciousness-raising, these women saw that their personal problems had political solutions.

I'm not claiming that every problem in a woman's life is the fault of the Patriarchy or 'the System'. Obviously, women—like men—can and often do make stupid decisions or act in dysfunctional ways; I have no argument with the idea that adults should take responsibility for their actions. What I'm claiming, when I invoke the Personal is Political ghost, is that members of an oppressed group have fewer and less attractive choices than non-oppressed people. Can members of either type of group mess things up for themselves? Of course, but we're not talking about *the decisions* of individuals, we're talking about the scope for decision-making that is available to individuals.

Throughout this book I analyse my own choices as well as those of men and women who have generously shared their experiences with me. I'm not offering examples of what to do or not do, how to live or think or cope. The individual stories I tell illustrate larger cultural patterns and examine different ways people negotiate these patterns. This includes the bits where I talk about me; I certainly haven't done so because I think my marriage or sex life or career goals are superior to anyone else's. Mine is just another life, another set of choices, some of which I've made as a conscious, striving feminist and some of which I've made as a flawed, hormone-driven and insecure mass of flesh and blood.

No story is supposed to be a warning or chastisement or prescription; they're all glimpses of lives and I hope readers will slot in their own experiences and ask questions. I don't expect readers to feel their personal choices are anyone's business but their own. What I care about is the fact that too many women are constrained in those choices because they are female. I care about that very much, and the stories in this book are told in an attempt to demonstrate why this is worth caring about.

A call to arms

In the first twenty years of the last century the suffragettes or first-wavers fought for—and eventually won—the right to vote and to be elected to public office. In the 1960s and 1970s, the second wave of the women's movement fought for—and mostly won—the right for women to control their own bodies and to train for and enter whatever occupation they chose. That women from all classes and racial backgrounds in many different parts of the developed world came together to form stunningly effective movements during these two periods was no accident.

The first wave was initiated in the US by women who had taken part in the abolition movement, and in the UK and Australia by women who had contributed to both the anti-war protest movement and the home-front war effort. The second wave emerged in response to the post-war attempts to return women to the domestic sphere and was informed by the politics and tactics of the civil rights and later, anti-war, movements.

The point of this potted history is that women's advances in terms of rights and social and political standing have never been the result of isolated actions of individual women making personal choices. And although feminism has frequently been about giving women the right to make any choice they want, it also recognises that choices are not made in a vacuum any more than movements grow in one.

I'm a writer, not an activist, but this book is, nevertheless, a call to arms. I wrote it because I've noticed that some lovely, hip, intelligent progressives, people who can recognise racial, religious and class-based oppression without difficulty, are uncomfortable with the idea that women in first-world countries face discrimination. I wrote it because I'm sick of hearing people say that women aren't oppressed because *their* husband does lots of housework or because *their* company pays women the same as men or because *they've* never personally been raped/groped/called a slut/been denied a basic human right.

I wrote this book because I believe people should not be defined solely by their sex. I believe legal, political and social forces limit the choices of women by insisting on defining them by their femaleness. I believe that by recognising and interrogating how gender roles operate in our culture we can begin to argue back, defy and confound. I believe that acknowledging the commonality of our experiences as women is the first and most important step to creating a society where we can think of ourselves in terms of character rather than gender.

This book is a call to arms for all the women who don't want to be defined only by their femaleness: to take the counter-intuitive step of talking about what they have in common with other women. And it's a call for men who are tired of the ridiculous battle-of-the-sexes crap: to start talking about the ways in which conformity to gender roles hurts them and the people they love. This isn't about joining some mythical sisterhood; it's about recognising that we need to act together to tackle sexism if we truly want to be free as individuals.

Women and men of my generation are beneficiaries of over a century of feminist thought and activism. The feminist project is by nature continuous because, as the culture and social landscape change, so too do the ways in which the movement and the culture intersect. The dazzling success of feminism has been due, in part, to the willingness of each succeeding generation to take the ideas and insights of their mothers and apply them to contemporary issues.

This book is my contribution to the conversation. In addition to the individual thinkers to whose ideas I refer and respond, I also want to acknowledge and thank the thousands of feminist theorists, writers, lobbyists, activists, reformers and leaders of the last hundred plus years. My personal feminism owes much to all of them and so does this book.

1
Your Vagina Is Not Like a Car

Who's a slut?

At my middle-class suburban high school a slut was a girl who wore eyeliner and rolled the waistband of her skirt. A slut spent her lunch hour smoking behind the basketball courts, trading dirty jokes and flirty looks with boys. A slut disappeared from a party with someone's older brother only to return an hour later with her hair dishevelled and her mascara smudged. A slut was me.

When I started being a slut I was fourteen years old and was still a virgin. Slut status did not depend on having sex but on people thinking that you did. I cultivated the reputation because it made boys less timid around me. Sometimes a boy would accuse me of holding out on him and nothing I could say would convince him that I'd already gone further with him than with anyone else. I experienced so many first times with boys who thought I was doing something out of habit. I loved the emotional privacy their assumptions afforded me.

I liked older boys better than boys my age, not because they were more interesting or sophisticated (they usually weren't) but because they were heavier, stronger and bolder. They ripped tights and sometimes shirts; their groping and nuzzling could bruise; their kisses left ugly red beard rashes. I liked walking away from an encounter marked. I know now that when most people see a teenage girl with bruised shins, dirty knees and chafed skin they think *poor kid* or *slut*. But when I was that girl, I walked tall. I felt beautiful and I felt good.

I know that doesn't sound right. I'm supposed to add that I had low self-esteem and was starved for attention and the only way I could feel powerful or wanted was by throwing myself at boys. But that's not true. I mean, sure, I thought I was fat and weird and that my parents didn't understand me, but I also knew I was smart and brave and that my parents didn't need to understand me to love me. I felt cared for and valued without the boys. With the boys, I felt *happy*.

You remember the kids at school who were super-athletic? After the cross-country or swimming carnival when everyone else was lying around exhausted, those kids would be grinning and glowing, as if they would like nothing more than to live the day over again. No one suggested they only liked sport because it made them feel powerful or popular, that they only worked so hard at winning because their parents ignored them or their uncle abused them. They did what made them feel alive and everybody cheered. Everybody except the sluts. We were back in the change-rooms doing what made us feel alive.

I'm not pretending that every experience I had was joyful and satisfying. Often, I felt physically uncomfortable and socially shamed. And I'm not going to claim that I felt respected, because I wasn't and I knew it. What I'm saying is that none of that mattered.

From primary school through to ninth grade I was a nerd and I wasn't respected or popular then either. No one ever told me not to study so hard or read so many books. No one said I should stop making a name for myself by topping all my classes. No one warned me to be careful or people would think of me as a brain rather than a whole person. I was happy living in my head, and so what if other people just knew me as 'the nerd'? And then I was happy living in my body and so what if people just knew me as 'the slut'?

Neither epithet had anything to do with who I was. I read and dreamt and studied and climbed into the backseats of older boys' cars. I didn't give a shit who said what, and I was right not to.

I don't extrapolate my experience to every girl who was 'easy' at school. I know some girls sleep around because they have no self-esteem or because they get drunk and don't know what they're doing or because they're desperate for love and attention. I know there are sad stories and that some girls and women use sex to fill gaping holes in their sense of self. But lots don't and that's my point: a woman's sexual behaviour, isolated from all other aspects of her personality, tells you nothing about who she is. A woman's sexual choices, isolated from all of her other choices, tell you nothing about what motivates her as a human being.

No one has called me a slut since high school. In my late teens I fell in love and by twenty I was a wife. My public image became profoundly respectable, but even had it not, even had my perceived promiscuity continued into my twenties, I would have been surprised to be called a slut. As a teenager, I heard the term slut almost every day, but almost never since. Outside of high school and American soap operas, people don't go around spitting insults in each others' faces, but this doesn't mean that the adult world is free of slut-naming and shaming.

Ask ten adults to define a slut and you'll hear things like: a woman who has sex with lots of men; a woman who sleeps around; a woman who has casual sex; a woman who flaunts her body. They'll probably also use words like loose, easy, trashy, cheap and desperate. Someone might say: a woman who has the sexual habits of a man. No one will say: a mythical creature dreamt up by people who are jealous of or threatened by female sexual expression.

Adult slut-shaming is most evident in the gossip rags and in moral panic opinion pieces that serve up the scandal for readers who think they're too sophisticated to read *Famous*. A Melbourne-based family therapist told the *Age* that the television show 'Big Brother' 'encourage[s] a sex culture'. The editor of the US gossip mag *Star* is quoted in the *New York Daily News* calling 2006 'the year of the slut' because it was dominated by 'party girls' like Britney Spears, Paris Hilton and Lindsay Lohan. A few months later, *Sydney Morning Herald* columnist Miranda Devine described Spears' 'exhibitionism, non-stop inebriation and casual couplings with numerous forgettable men' as 'self-destructive slutty behaviour' that should not be considered the 'natural reaction of a young woman letting down her hair after a marriage breakdown'.

With the heading 'Girls Gone Bad' *Newsweek* fretted that the antics of Hilton, Spears and Lohan may be turning girls into 'prosti-tots'. Yes, under the banner of concern we can get away with calling kids who emulate popstars and models 'whores'. That article quotes a fifth-grade teacher approving of the fact her students call Spears a 'hootch'.

In the *Age*, a sports writer jokes that for cricketers, 'getting sledged by the Australians is probably a bit like Paris Hilton—eventually everybody gets a turn'. That's as hilarious as those town bike jokes back at high school. Funnier still was the gag made by MSNBC newscaster Keith Olbermann, who, by the way, is widely considered progressive and therefore not expected to come out with sexist bile. 'Paris Hilton claims she was punched in the face yesterday morning at a nightclub in Hollywood,' Olbermann said. After pausing for effect, he let the zinger fly: 'Course she's had worse things happen to her face ...'

The joke, if you missed it, is that maybe Hilton's had man parts or even man *juice* on her face, which means she's had sex which is way, way worse than getting punched! Consensual sex is worse than getting belted, right? And in case you think I'm somehow misinterpreting his comment, the line at the bottom of the screen was the delightfully witty play on words: 'A Slut and Battery'. Get it? Assault and battery is hilarious if it happens to a slut.

Now, say all you want about how shallow and spoilt Hilton, Spears and friends are, and I'm with you, nodding along. But start slut-shaming them and we've got a problem. What these young women do or don't do with their genitals is beside any legitimate, non-sexist point you could make. There may be something wrong with being a cheerleader for shallow celebrity culture; there's nothing wrong with having lots of sex. There's nothing wrong with critiquing the influence these young celebrities have on their fans; there's something very, very wrong about suggesting that violence against such women is less serious because they are (or appear to be) sexually promiscuous.

Beyond the world of celebrity gossip, slut-shaming tends to be less overt, but that's because the behaviour of non-famous women is not reported in tabloids. If your neighbour goes out without knickers, it's unlikely a photographer will be waiting with camera angled upwards for the moment she climbs out of her car. Likewise, if your workmate makes a sex tape it's probably not going to become the most requested download on YouTube. If the 'sluttish' behaviour is less public, then so is the censure and shaming. Real-life adult slut-shaming tends to be of the condescending variety that pretends to be concerned.

According to TV, movies, women's magazines and pop psychology, women who 'sleep around' do so because they have low self-esteem, a drug or alcohol problem, father issues, mother issues, body issues or depression. A *USA Today* opinion piece titled 'A Neo-feminist's View of Abstinence' described the tragedy in store for women who have sex before marriage:

> Things go 'great' for a month or two. Sex quickly becomes a part of your interactions. Maybe he even meets your parents. And then, well, things just change. He dumps you or you dump him. Regardless of why the relationship died, you are now one of many women whom he could point out on the street. 'See her?' he can tell his buddies. 'She's cute, huh? Yeah, I had her.' I never want to be 'her'.

The writer, Elizabeth Sandoval, says nothing about the behaviour of the man who points out women he's 'had'. 'Women are non-self-respecting,' she writes further, 'because they willingly sacrifice such an important part of their being for just a few moments of pleasure.' No, no, *no*. Non-self-respecting is thinking that all you deserve is a 'few moments of pleasure'. Non-self-respecting is to sleep with the kind of man who'd brag about his sexual conquests to all his buddies, but only after you've married him, so *you* won't be one of those bragged-about conquests.

A self-described 'hard-core Christian' told me that women sleep around because 'the feminists told them they should', while a hard-core feminist told me that they do it because 'sex is a way of gaining power and women have so little that you can't blame them for trying to get it any way they can'. Only when I asked a woman who, in her own words, 'gets off with loads of blokes' did I hear an answer that did not use the vocabulary of addiction or psychiatric trouble.

'I like sex,' Natalie tells me. 'Sometimes, okay, often, I meet a man and my mind automatically jumps to what he'd be like in bed. If he's single, I don't see why I shouldn't try and answer that question.'

She shrugs. 'It's weird. Even [she names a friend who's marched in the Sydney Gay and Lesbian Mardi Gras since she was fifteen] got all serious on me last week. I mentioned this lovely bloke I'd gone home with the night before and she was all "I hope you're being careful. I just want you to find happiness". I felt like she'd misheard me. It was like I'd confessed to having a heroin habit instead of an orgasm.'

Does it worry her that people—even friends—think of her as troubled or damaged?

'Sometimes. Sometimes I think there is something wrong with me. Not because I have lots of sex, but because it doesn't make me feel bad. I'm healthy. I mean, I'm careful about my health. And I'm not lonely or bored or sad. I mean, sometimes I'm sad but it's for the normal reasons—death and war and stuff. Sometimes,' she smiles and covers her face for a second, 'if I'm honest, the thing that makes me feel worst is that I'll never be able to sleep with all the blokes I'd like to.' She laughs. 'There are just so many lovely blokes in the world, I'll never get to them all!'

Natalie also gives me the perfect definition.

'A slut,' she says, 'is just a woman who has more sex or more sexual partners than whoever is doing the labelling thinks she should.'

What's so bad about being a slut?

So, okay, we have a workable definition of the word 'slut', but the real question, the interesting and important question, is why is promiscuity (however it is defined) such a bad thing? Why is experience—something that often makes a person more accomplished—a negative thing when it comes to sex? Why do rational adults suddenly turn into concerned old maiden aunts or lemon-mouthed little kids when it comes to talking about a woman who's had lots (whatever that means) of lovers?

The answer, sadly, is that many people believe that a woman's sexuality is a limited resource. Curt Smith is the 'relationship correspondent' for *AskMen.com*, an online magazine which claims a monthly readership of six million and a 34 percent share of the men's online lifestyle market. Curt had the following to say about a woman who wrote to him asking why her boyfriend had left her after discovering she'd had lots of lovers:

> An object that has value is worshipped, respected, cherished, and shared with very few deserving people. As soon as you start sharing

that object with anyone and without care, the object starts to lose value. The more people use the object, the more it depreciates and the less bargaining power it has: this is a plain psychological fact of life.

Curt uses a cute analogy to illustrate his point: 'If I were to offer Stacy the same engagement ring that I once offered my ex-fiancée, would she appreciate it? I'm sure she wouldn't, and it's only a ring. Then how do you think men feel when a woman offers herself once she's already offered it to so many other men?' I'm not sure if the 'it' to which Curt refers is a woman's vagina, a woman's entire body or the unquantifiable substance of a woman's sexuality, but either way his is a creepy, misogynous view of what should be a mutual exchange of pleasure.

It is also a common one in the world of relationship and dating advice. Depending on who is doing the comparing, a woman (or, more specifically, a vagina) is either like a battery (can only be used so many times before it runs out) or a car (value decreases with use). Even ignoring the offensive connotations of woman as a tradeable commodity, these kind of analogies are ridiculous because they rest on the idea that a vagina has a severely limited life span. Anyone who has, or has had, an extended relationship with a vagina knows this is nonsense.

Think about the popular insult 'loose'. Why might this phrase refer to a woman who has lots of sex? Sex does not loosen or otherwise alter the shape or muscle tone of the vagina. If anything, lots of (good) sex will result in tighter muscles due to all those lovely orgasmic contractions. A penis, even a larger than average penis, is simply not large enough to permanently stretch the vaginal walls.

Another common theory about promiscuous females is that they are riddled with sexually transmitted infections. It's always made sense to me that experienced players would be more likely to be aware of the various risks associated with sexual activity and to know how to minimise if not avoid such risks. A study by the London School of Hygiene and Tropical Medicine, which appeared in the *Lancet* in November 2006, confirms my assumptions. The study of sexual behaviour in fifty-nine countries found women in industrialised countries had more sexual partners than those in developing nations but had lower rates of sexually transmitted diseases and infections. Sexually transmitted infections were more common in societies in which women were sexually oppressed or unable to negotiate with sexual partners for condom use or other precautions.

So what, if not biology or anatomy, is behind our culture's hatred and disgust for the promiscuous woman? This is where we return to the idea of female sexuality as a commodity. In a society that views her sexuality as a resource to be bought, sold and bartered, a woman who 'gives it away' is devaluing the product. A 'cheap' woman has the same effect on the sex market as a budget airline has on airfares. Men can't be expected to 'pay' for sex by buying dinners and diamond rings and a three-bedroom house in the suburbs, when they can get the same 'product' from the neighbourhood slut for free.

Does this sound too cynical? Too simplistic? Like I'm stuck in 1955? I know, I feel like that too sometimes. I keep hearing that it's all in the past, this stuff about men wanting sex all the time and women making them work for it. About men using love to get sex and women using sex to get love. I'm told we're in a sex-positive, liberated era now, you know, because of Samantha in 'Sex and the

City' and other fictional characters.

Just because a made-up chick on a TV show has lots of sex doesn't mean mainstream social attitudes to female sexuality have changed. Back to the wise Curt Smith and *AskMen.com*:

> There used to be a time when women could signal to a man, 'If you stay with me, I'll let you have my body.' But now men are saying, 'It's okay, you can keep it because with all this supply, it's just not worth as much as it once was.' That's why today, we find a lot of women complaining that men no longer want to commit. This is false; men still want to commit, but women no longer have that special gift to bait men into a relationship.

Bait men into a relationship! If it were only online advice columnists spouting this kind of stuff there wouldn't be so much cause for concern, but mainstream publications are printing the same crap. Aussie women's magazine *Madison*, for example, recently published an extract from Kate Taylor's *Not Tonight Mr Right*, in which she argued: 'if you want to establish the most secure and long-lasting relationship you've ever had—a relationship that is fun, blissfully happy, and fills you with a sense of peace—all you have to do is not have sex with him.'

Romance is ruining your sex life

Columnist Miranda Devine takes the behaviour of Spears, Hilton and Co as reflecting a wider cultural problem. 'Mutual respect between the sexes, romance and a legacy of chivalry by men entranced by the feminine mystique have been trashed in the name of female equality and sexual liberation,' she rants. 'When women treat themselves like sluts why would men treat them any differently?' She finishes by calling on women to 'seize back their inner prude'.

First of all, *mutual* respect is exactly the point here. Why no chagrin for the male counterparts of Britney and friends? Second, women who have sex without regard to the sensitivities of this sort of newspaper columnist do not treat themselves like sluts. They treat themselves like adult women who want to have sex.

As to the 'romance and chivalry' thing, this is an increasingly popular line of attack for people who want to restrict the freedoms of women. A recent article by Laura Sessions Stepp in the *Washington Post* lamented that young women were 'hooking up'—defined as anything from kissing to having sex—rather than forming long-term relationships. The problem, according to Stepp, is that women become all sad and used and no man wants to marry a sad, used girl. Stepp's book, *Unhooked: How Young Women Pursue Sex, Delay Love, and Lose at Both*, uses a charming analogy: 'In a smorgasbord of booty, all the hot dishes start looking like they've been on the warming table too long.' (And the lukewarm plate of food beats cars and batteries in the competition for dodgiest slut analogy.) Neither article nor book mentions the party boys or the male partners of the hook-up girls. The derision and panic is all about the sexual behaviour of girls.

Again, focusing on the behaviour of women, research from Sheffield University, presented at the 2006 British Psychological Society Conference, found that 90 percent of surveyed women considered casual sex 'wrong' and thought that 'women engaging in casual sex were seen as trying to be like men'. Now let's just contemplate this expression 'trying to be like men'; it comes up a lot when discussing the whole slut thing. 'Trying to be like a man' or 'having sex like a man' means having casual sex or sex that is purely physical. This sort of expression unfairly and inaccurately labels promiscuity and hard-heartedness as male attributes and primness and emotionality as female. When you hear someone say a woman has sex like a man, you're hearing an expression of contempt for the woman (she's a slut) and for men (sex is never emotional or important to them).

I blame a certain idea of romance. I'm talking about flowers and chocolates, diamonds are forever romance. I'm talking about romance as a culture, as a way of thinking about gender relations. This romance is about a boy loving a girl so much he spends all his money on her which makes her so, so happy that she has sex with him—which is the female equivalent of spending all one's money, because everybody knows that a vagina equals personal worth.

Believing in this kind of romance means believing that women have sex for love and men use love to get sex. It says women's hearts are connected to their ring fingers which, once activated with a sparkly stone, connect to their clitorises and therefore truly rewarding sex can only happen if heart and ring finger are satisfied first. It says that the girl with the biggest diamond wins.

This damaging kind of romantic idealism says that a girl worth loving will resist and resist, and a boy worth loving will push and push. The happy ending comes when his manly not-taking-no-for-an-answer wins and she whimperingly submits. Stalking, abduction and date rape used to be considered romantic. (See for instance, *Seven Brides for Seven Brothers*, 'General Hospital's' Luke and Laura, *Overboard* and *Gone with the Wind.*)

Nowadays people are hip to the idea that no means no and so the correct way to break her resistance (and she will be resistant—she's female, remember?) is to do the washing up, light candles, rub her feet, buy her dinner, tell her she's the most beautiful creature on earth, because, as readers of relationship advice columns know, women need to feel relaxed, special and secure before they can enjoy sex. Men, presumably, enjoy sex even when feeling tense, ordinary and in danger. Or maybe it's that men, being the dominant cultural force and all, already feel relaxed, special and secure and therefore need no lighting-of-sacred-sexy-wax-sticks and rubbing-of-tired-downtrodden-feet before getting right into the good stuff. Or maybe the whole thing is a load of crap.

Advice columnists and feature writers never pause to consider how *un*special a woman feels when she knows a bloke is just going through the motions in order for her to feel *relaxed* enough to get off. Here's the scoop: some women like candles and foot rubs followed by languorous, full-eye-contact love-making; some women like fast, impersonal fucking in public toilet blocks; some women like both; most women like eight million things that lie between these two extremes; so do most men. If you're a man who wants to have sex with a woman, then for God's sake think about the woman you want to have sex with, not some generic nice-girl-who-loves-flowers-and-soft-tender-kisses or town-slut-who-hates-herself-but-loves-screwing-mean-men.

The Nice Girls Don't scenario hurts women who enjoy sex by labelling them sluts, but it also hurts women who *don't* enjoy sex by encouraging the view that they're not supposed to. According to this logic, only sluts enjoy it enough to do it for free, because they want to. And if you never orgasm or you feel uncomfortable about something your boyfriend is doing or you spend intimate time with your husband mentally making a shopping list, it means you are a normal, healthy woman. You are having sex to make him happy so that he will do things that make *you* happy later. It's a straightforward exchange, and enjoyment is beside the point. Why do so many women continue to accept a lack of sexual satisfaction as normal, given that they have been blessed with an organ—the clitoris—whose sole purpose is sexual pleasure?

This attitude hurts men, too. A man I know 'went right off' a girl he'd been head over heels for after he found out she'd had what he considered 'heaps' of lovers. I admitted confusion. The girl was smart, attractive and reportedly 'fantastic' in bed. What difference did it make how many blokes she'd had sex with?

'I just feel like I'm not that important to her,' he said. 'Other girls I've been with, I knew they were totally into me because they wouldn't have slept with me otherwise. With Kate, I realised she might be just having a bit of fun with me.'

I felt for him, really. It's awful not to know if the object of your affections is as invested in the relationship as you are. But if you want a relationship with someone, you must—at some point—learn to talk to them about this stuff and be able to trust what they tell you. My friend didn't ask dream-girl/slut-girl if she was serious about him. He didn't tell her he was serious about her. He just found out she'd had sex with lots of men and then skedaddled, because he thought that there must be something insincere about a girl who has sex because she likes it. Buying into the myth that women don't enjoy sex as much as men caused my friend to end a potentially fulfilling relationship with someone whose company he enjoyed.

So much of the battle-of-the-sexes nonsense that goes on in our society is a result of this kind of Jane Austenesque gender-exclusive ignorance. Men believe women don't really like sex, they complain about it to their mates, they contrive ways to convince the women in their lives to go to bed with them, and they lament the unfairness of having to work so hard just to get laid. And then they meet a woman who's totally into it, and they collapse into misery and confusion. *What could it mean that she wants to have sex with me when I haven't even said I love her? Does this mean she will really like having sex with other men, that I am not the only penis-owner who can satisfy her?* And women play along, going home frustrated every night because he hasn't performed enough money-spending, movie-romance rituals to allow her to sleep with him without feeling like a 'slut'. Or they stop playing the game, sleep with whomever they want whenever they want, and end up stigmatised or pitied.

Imagine if we taught girls that sex is supposed to be pleasurable. Imagine if we taught boys that girls were as interested in sex as they are. Imagine if we taught that sex is something men and women do because they want to. Imagine if we gave young people the knowledge and tools and confidence to have only the kind of sex they enjoy with people they like when they feel like it. The power of the slut insult disappears. *She's done it with loads of guys!* Wow, she must be good at it. *She can't get enough!* Well, who can?

2
Princesses, Popstars and the Rest of Us

The princesses

Around four thousand Australian women auditioned for a place on the first series of the execrable reality TV show 'Australian Princess'. Despite the intense bagging the show received, Channel 10 commissioned a second series, for which even more women turned out to audition. 'Australian Princess' followed in the cringe-worthy footsteps of Cinderella TV classics such as 'Extreme Makeover', 'The Swan' (in which women were subjected to cosmetic surgery and bullying from various 'experts' until their perceived imperfections had been eliminated), 'The Bachelor' and 'Joe Millionaire' (in which a harem of pretty young women competed for the 'honour' of being chosen by a single man).

The specifics of 'Australian Princess' are that 'a team of international experts in etiquette and the royal pursuits' led by former royal butler Paul Burrell (the man Princess Di described as 'her rock' and who repaid her trust and devotion by writing a gossipy book about her) will teach average girls 'all the skills required in order to fit into proper society'.

Putting aside the question of whether anyone thinks that inbreeding, obscene wealth and an obsession with hats and table manners constitute 'proper society', why on earth would anyone want to be part of that society? Along with the royal title come a lifetime of sacrifice and a reduction in personal autonomy. Princess Mary of Denmark, for example, had to lose weight, take deportment and elocution lessons and have media training. She also converted to the Lutheran faith, relinquished her nationality and agreed to surrender custody of any future children in the case of divorce.

All this makes Mary a perfect fit for the cult of the princess. Transformation, rather than the woman herself, is at the heart of the story. The agents of transformation, whether fairy godmothers or elocution coaches, are the ones driving the action. Before she has even married her prince, the princess has abdicated responsibility for herself. She wears what she is told and imitates her mentors in speech and behaviour. And although the story ends with the princess triumphantly rolling man-putty in her French-manicured hands, her power is as ephemeral as a pumpkin coach. It has been granted by others and can be taken away by same.

The life, death and afterlife of Princess Diana demonstrate how this works. With the assistance of expensive stylists, royal advisors and the media, the pretty nineteen-year-old with a shy smile became a glamorous and adored princess. A decade later, the royal family and media withdrew their support and the tiara was promptly plucked from her no longer regal head.

Once they'd found the princess was fallible and the disappointment of the masses had faded, the elements that turned the media against her became what the public valued most. Her bulimia, low self-esteem, ill-fated affairs with unsuitable men and her struggle for independence resonated with many women. The fact she had gone through so many ordinary traumas and come out the other side stronger and more confident made her a realistic role model for ordinary women, which is something a princess could never be.

Then, just as Diana seemed to have broken free of her role as 'princess', she died and was reclaimed by the royals. Prince Charles collected her body from Paris and escorted it to London, and her funeral cortege was followed by Windsor men, while her sisters and mother waited in the church. The media largely supported the post-mortem rehabilitation of Princess Diana, and those who had, in life, taunted and hounded her, spoke of her with respect and admiration. With Prime Minister Tony Blair's use of the phrase 'the people's princess' the reverse was complete: Diana was a perfect princess once more. Her second coronation had as little to do with her as a person as the first.

None of the 'Australian Princess' entrants is ever going to join the ranks of royalty, and so the trials of literal princesshood are not an issue. In fact, aside from the title and a couple of cameos by minor European royals, 'Australian Princess' is a decidedly un-regal affair. The wannabe princesses of season one knew nothing of royalty beyond 'poor Diana', 'sexy William' and 'our Mary'. They'd not heard of Sarah Ferguson and struggled to identify a photograph of the Queen Mother. They complained constantly about etiquette training—although with lessons such as 'how to eat a banana politely' (use a knife and fork so as not to look like a pornstar) who can blame them—and they expressed frustration with the heels, pantyhose and make-up they were forced to wear. The prospect of a trip to England was exciting; the promise of dancing with an actual prince left them cold. All wanted desperately to win the title of Australian Princess but none wanted to do anything that a real princess might.

The solution to this seeming paradox is that for the contestants the role of 'princess' is a life choice, not a job description. Witness season two contestant Leanne Churchill who undermines the whole premise of the show by declaring that, 'every girl is a princess!' Or fellow princess-in-training Stephanie Jenkinson who says that, 'everyone qualifies to be a princess'. This is apparently true: host Jackie O, best known as one half of a prank-calling Top 40 radio show, is, according to the show's promo material, a 'media princess'.

The belief that 'every woman is a princess if she says she is' goes far beyond TV land. 'She's my little princess,' a father says, even though he would never dream of sending his daughter to deportment lessons. 'He makes me feel like a princess,' a young woman may say of her lover, but she means that he spoils her with foot massages, not that he insists she take a fertility test before he will marry her. 'I felt like a princess,' a teenager tells a reporter for the *Age*, referring to her debutante ball.

T-shirts bearing slogans such as 'Bow to the Princess' and 'It's Not Easy Being a Princess' are a common sight on campuses and in shopping centres, and gold-painted tin tiaras adorned with coloured glass jewels are popular evening accessories. To the modern girl being a princess is about being pretty, pampered and protected.

'My boyfriend treats me like a princess,' says a twenty-year-old student of mine who, like her friends, is always immaculately made-up and expensively dressed. I ask her to elaborate.

'He buys me little presents, pays when we go out. He paid my car registration for me.'

'Only because you spent the rego money on shoes,' her friend interjects.

'He pretended to be annoyed,' says the Suburban Princess, 'but I know he liked doing it. He likes taking care of me.'

With this boast, my student demonstrated what lies beneath the phenomenon of princess culture. A princess wants, or believes she needs, a man to protect her, not necessarily from physical harm, but from hard work, drudgery and responsibility.

As with most cultural infections, princesshood starts young. Check out the toy section of any department store and you will find aisles swathed and merchandised in princess pink. The bulk of the items for sale will most likely be from Disney's Princess range, which, in keeping with the 'every girl is a princess' trope, includes such non-regal heroines as Mulan and Pocahontas. (The Mulan Princess doll smilingly wears the movement-restricting kimono hated and joyfully discarded by the non-princess heroine of the movie.) And for when a girl outgrows dolls and is ready to marry the prince and set up castle for herself, Disney has released a collection of bridal gowns inspired by Cinderella, Sleeping Beauty, Snow White, Belle, Jasmine and Ariel.

Being a self-described princess is cute in a four-year-old, irritating in an older kid and creepy in an adult woman. This is not simply a matter of taste; it's not that I have an aversion to pink satin and want to ensure no woman ever wears it again. Princess culture is disturbing because of what it does to girls and women who are seduced by the promise of a happy-ever-after result as long as they follow the rules. The rules are easy to figure out—read any glossy women's magazine or watch 'Sex and the City', 'Desperate Housewives' or anything from the Cinderella TV genre.

'If you want to be a princess,' says Jean Broke-Smith, 'Australian Princess' etiquette expert, 'the most important thing is that you're on duty from the moment you get up in the morning. You need to be in control at all times…' Control means speaking quietly and only after first mentally rehearsing your words. It means cutting out your own tongue rather than becoming argumentative or passionate. It means accepting that it is more important to make others comfortable than to make them think or understand. And after you have wrestled your personality into submission it means a lifetime of obsessing over surface and detail. An elegant bag, unique vase or lightly perfumed hand-written thankyou note will create the illusion that you are an individual with ideas of your own.

Commenting on the upswing in popularity of debutante balls in Australia, Monash University's Leslie Cannold told the *Age*, 'there is perhaps a sense among young women that by doing it "properly", and by that I mean traditionally, it somehow immunises them against divorce.' And, in the end, that's what's really awful about modern princesshood. Even if a girl does everything 'properly', even if she succeeds in her quest (unlikely, given the dullness that must be endured and the dearth of unattached princes) she can't be anything but disappointed. In princessland nothing that binds or rips apart real relationships exists.

There is no politics or religion or family, no housework or illness or grief. It is a world where love, sex and marriage have no context, no real meaning and a fairytale wedding heralds The End.

The popstars

The fascination with princesses is not new: before Diana and Mary, the women's magazines were obsessed by Grace, Stephanie, Caroline and Margaret. The desire to be a princess, to take on that ultra-feminine role of the pampered and protected, is even older, which is what makes the current cult so frustrating. Shouldn't we be over this by now?

Sadly, the princess thing is part of a larger popular culture trend towards old-fashioned gender role pigeonholing disguised as sassy female empowerment. It seems the more that women infiltrate the professional and political realms and the better that girls perform in school and university, the more retrograde that pop culture representations of women become.

Back in the mid-1990s, a time which now appears progressive, I was a middle-class suburban adolescent in thrall, like every other girl I knew, to angsty, would-be-alternative singer, Alanis Morissette. We knew every word of every song on *Jagged Little Pill* and we sang (or yelled) along with all our teenaged passion. When Morissette wailed 'you took me out to wine, dine, sixty-nine me but didn't hear a damn word I said' we knew her anger was righteous and that it was ours. A couple of years earlier Salt 'n' Pepa's 'None of your Business' was an anthem amongst the 'nice girls' I knew: 'How many rules am I to break before you understand that your double-standards don't mean shit to me?' we shouted and we meant it even though we didn't always live it.

We were rebelling in a time-honoured way—through the safety of pop music. Although it is clear now that we were singing of our ownership of our bodies and lives, we didn't consider these songs feminist or empowering—they simply spoke to us. Indeed, if one wanted feminist music there was plenty of it around in the nineties, but not in my world, not in the world of school disco DJs, Saturday morning 'Video Hits' and commercial FM radio.

Today, feminist music is practically a genre in itself, but none of it seems to have crept into the mainstream. Many teenage girls listen only to Top 40 tunes, like those of the Black-Eyed Peas, whose 'My Humps' celebrates a woman's ability to extort money from men using her 'lovely lady lumps' or the Pussycat Dolls, whose 'Don't Cha', contains the line 'Don't cha wish your girlfriend was hot like me'. These songs happen to be top of the charts as I write, but I could have picked almost any hit by a female singer from any mainstream music chart of the last few years and found similar sentiments. Such songs are, needless to say, often accompanied by video clips that can only be described as soft porn.

It may not be apparent how explicit lyrics, coupled with groin-grinding dance moves by women in their underwear, could be considered 'conservative'. But look a little deeper and it becomes clear that the gender politics are circa 1950.

The Pussycat Dolls have a Cinderella TV show of their own, 'Pussycat Dolls Present: The Search for the Next Doll', described by the producer as 'empowering' and part of 'third-wave feminism'. The group's founder echoes the 'every girl is a princess' sentiment, saying that 'getting up there and dressing like a Doll' is something that 'inside, every girl in the world wants to do'.

Today's mainstream pop acts reveal a serious confusion. The abilities and competence of women are acknowledged by their presence centre stage, but their authority is undermined by the sheer submissiveness of their lyrics. The oiled-up, pelvis-thrusting, money-extorting music video 'ho' is the ideological twin of the tea-making, polite small-talking, pink Chanel-suit-wearing modern-day princess.

The rest of us (or the problem with femininity)

Princess culture and the hyper-sexualised gender roles of the popular music scene are connected by their message: the best way for a woman to get by in life is to cater to male desires. These gender roles are products of popular culture and thus tend to focus on a particular demographic of women: the young and aspirational middle class. But even women who fall outside of this group—the over thirties, the working class, the cultural rebels, those who don't watch TV or listen to mainstream music or read fashion magazines—are susceptible to the message that being female is a condition that must be modified by masks, poses and practised behaviours.

I'm talking about the cult of femininity, which influences every woman and girl living in western societies. Note that 'femininity' and 'feminine' are not interchangeable with 'femaleness' or 'female'. The latter terms refer to biological sex, something that can't be altered without surgery and massive doses of hormones. Femininity on the other hand refers to a set of learned and culturally specific behaviours. Femaleness is morally and politically neutral. Femininity is not.

Femininity describes all those things women do to conform to the socially accepted model of femaleness. At the mild end we're talking about lipstick and skirts; at the extreme, labioplasty and breast enlargement; in between, stilettos and genital waxing.

For all its girl-power pop songs and 'princesses rule' T-shirts, our culture takes a harsh view of women who don't work to obtain the feminine norm. We are taught to feel ashamed of our bodies in their natural state. Leg and underarm hair? Gross. Breasts that are not lifted and separated by wire and Spandex? Embarrassing. A female face without make-up? Ugly. Femaleness in its natural form is so revolting that women must embrace the cult of femininity in order to be acceptable. To refuse to shave, wax, suck in, push out, paint and cover in the prescribed ways is to risk being identified as a creature unworthy of respectful treatment, being labelled a pig, a cow, a dog, being shoved into the category of radical, dyke, ugly, masculine, bitch. To be unfeminine is to risk being unemployable, unheard, untouchable, unfuckable.

And so, even though it's expensive and time-consuming and frequently uncomfortable if not downright painful, we go along with it. Even those of us who have not internalised the message that we are naturally unattractive go along with this feminine reprogramming because not to do it means making a daily statement about our resistance to cultural norms. Most of us are too occupied with the business of living our lives to want to fight that battle every day.

For example, I used to teach critical thinking and writing to a group of highly image-conscious older teens. When I stood in front of that class I didn't want my students to see a militant, mannish feminazi (their interpretation of un-feminised women, not mine), because perceiving me that way would make it harder for them to hear what I was saying. Had I feminised myself to the point of movie-star glamour they would've been equally distracted, perceiving me to be a creature of beauty and charm rather than intellect.

So, precariously, I feminised myself to a point where I judged my students would not note my appearance at all. I chose clothing that was somewhere between androgynous and girlish, 'natural-looking' make-up and low heels. I'd have been more comfortable in flat shoes and more productive without the done-but-not-overdone make-up, but I'm a realist and I knew that dressing to blend in would make my real work easier.

I was not following an official dress code, merely attempting to mute and blur the messages my students received from my appearance. After asking some friends about how they decide on work-appropriate clothing, I was reminded that my ability to control how I presented myself at that teaching job placed me in a feminist paradise compared to many working women.

I say 'reminded' because I could recall my experiences during the years I worked for several major corporations. I could remember the regulation-fitted just-below-the-knee skirts that women referred to as the 'rapist's friend', because they made it impossible to either run or kick, skills which women traversing train stations and car parks at night may well need. I remembered the way that the required skin-tone pantyhose made sweaty summer legs itch and turn red. I remembered having to ask a male co-worker for help in lifting what should have been a perfectly manageable box of files, because my darted, fitted jacket restricted my range of movement.

My experiences were all between five and ten years ago, and many middle and lower level corporate women still have to follow dress codes which differ from those of male colleagues. The code for administrative staff at a certain IT company requires women to wear 'stockings or pantyhose', and 'heeled shoes' if wearing a skirt, and 'shoes with heels' if wearing pants. No 'undergarments' should be visible through clothing. Male and female sales staff at a major telecommunications company are required to wear business suits, with the added note to female employees of 'skirt suits only, NO trousers'. A friend who works in a local government office says, despite adhering to the 'well-groomed and professional' guidelines, she was advised by a manager to 'put on some lipstick and blush' before meeting with clients.

Marie Claire in June 2007 reported on UK research that indicated 'a quarter of employers admitted they were more likely to hire a woman who wore make-up than one who didn't'. In the feature, entitled 'How Does Your Make-up Affect Your Career?', the magazine tested the findings for itself, by presenting a woman in six make-up guises, 'from underplayed to overstated', to a panel of recruitment 'experts'. With no make-up and tied back hair, she was given a combined score of 12/30. With lots of make-up her score was only slightly better: 14/30. The 'winning look', with a score of 27/30, was one with blow-dried hair, visible eye make-up and lipstick. It's probably unnecessary to add that there was no hair and make-up test for prospective male employees.

One would hope that once a woman got to a certain level of power and esteem in the corporate world, the focus on her appearance would ease. One would be wrong. The extra time and expense required for women to appear well groomed in a professional context in fact appears to increase the higher up the corporate ladder a woman rises.

Michelle, who is the only woman on the senior management team of a major property investment corporation, tells me that she spends more money on her work wardrobe than men in similar positions 'as women's suits tend to be as expensive but change every season whereas men's are pretty much the same, and you can buy well cut suits for men at a range of price points'. She also points out that the many corporate functions, particularly black tie and cocktail events, that executives are expected to attend, require women to spend yet more time and money on their appearance. 'You can't wear a suit so you need to come up with something which is appropriate yet professional...Most evening clothes are too frivolous or too revealing to wear to a work function.'

If the workplace is a tough environment for the femininity-resistant woman, the social world is worse. I can't recall a single social event I've attended in my life at which there was not a conversation about the way the women and girls were dressed and/or groomed. Who had a new hairstyle, who had lost or put on weight, where someone bought her shoes, how much those earrings cost. A woman I know who has an education level and professional status far beyond that of anyone in her family was 'affectionately' bullied by that same 'proud, loving family' into losing fifteen kilos off her size 12 frame. Nowadays she spends at least an hour in the gym every day even if that means getting up before dawn, missing a lunch with friends or getting home after her husband has gone to bed. Another awesome feminist woman I know (okay, it's me) sometimes wears a pair of boots that make her feet ooze blood because those boots make her short, stumpy legs look long and thin.

Women do expensive, time-consuming, painful things in order to meet some arbitrary, culturally defined standard of 'beauty' for the same reason they get up early in order to paint their faces for work: it prevents them from being labelled as outsiders (dyke, femi-nazi, radical, hippy, butch) and bestows upon them advantages and rewards that would not otherwise be available. For every behaviour considered 'feminine' there is a corresponding benefit, and a disadvantage for those women who refuse to comply.

The fact that women who meet society's standards of beauty are paid more, promoted sooner and treated more respectfully is a media cliché. Giving well-meaning advice to women who don't meet those standards (Dress for Success! Embrace your Inner Sex Symbol! Slim your way to a Better Job! Don't Let Bad Hair Get You Down!) is the women's magazine's *raison d'être*.

To be clear, I am not blaming individual women for going along with this. It makes a lot of sense to act in whatever way provides the most benefits. These strategies have saved a lot of women from a lot of hard work, and given them advantages over less successfully feminine women. If society sees you primarily as either a womb or a sex-object then it makes sense to be the best womb/sex-object you can. Then you'll perhaps gain the power/wealth/independence otherwise denied you on the grounds of gender.

But the problem is that although what used to be called 'feminine wiles' may help individual women gain advantage in an unfair system, they hurt the larger cause of equality. It's like the princesses and booty-shakers: the individual may gain power or privilege but the system that has taken away that power and privilege in the first place is reinforced.

Yes, I know you sometimes feel unbelievably sexy after a bikini wax and spray tan. I understand you emerge feeling like a goddess after a day spent shopping and pampering. I'm not ashamed to admit that wearing my blood-drawing boots makes me feel gorgeous (in a crippled kind of way). You will never hear me say that a person should stop engaging in beauty or fashion-related behaviour that makes her feel good. You will hear me say that we feel hot after doing these things because the culture tells us that this is what hot is, and does, and looks like.

Every culture has versions of sexual attractiveness and it's next to impossible to avoid being influenced by them. But if you can feel attractive only after spending six hours in the beauty salon and three hours with the hair stylist, after applying several chemical formulas to your face, after slipping into underwear that restricts your breathing and shoes that make it difficult to walk, then you have become a slave to the culture. Go ahead and have a Brazilian, but if you feel powerful afterwards, ask yourself where that power originates. If it is, as I suspect, from making a grown man your willing sex slave, be aware that the power—though enjoyable—is something he has briefly given to you because you have conformed to a standard that pleases him. When you stop pleasing him, the power goes away too.

And if how sexy you feel is only related to how much you conform to someone else's version of what sexy *looks like*, then you are—by definition—a sex-object. Most of us have been sex-objects at one time or another, perhaps without knowing it, because it's a matter of how another person sees us. This is all part of messy, confusing, fabulous sexual attraction. But if you see *yourself* as the sex-object, if you can only enjoy sex when you think you look like someone with whom other people will enjoy sex, if feeling sexy is about the lingerie you're wearing rather than the way your nerve endings are tingling, then you are performing sex rather than experiencing it.

(An aside to the heterosexual men protesting that they 'can't help being attracted to ultra-groomed, pubeless, lipsticked women': if women (all women) simply stopped shaving, plucking, waxing, lipsticking and hair-dyeing, my bet is that love and sex would still happen. Marriages would still be made and broken. Babies would still be conceived. Men would still get erections and feel the desire to put them inside the bodies of women with hairy legs and armpits.)

I wish I could make all this sound less holier-than-thou. I am complicit in the cult of femininity and my preachy tone is the same one I use with myself every day. I am aware that I adopt many feminine behaviours because I don't want to fall too far outside the mainstream standards of 'attractive', standards that derive from centuries of women being treated as sex-objects and domestic decorations. Most of the time I want to fit those standards enough so that I can go about my life without being challenged or disapproved of before I even open my mouth.

3
Girls Gone Wild vs. Girls Gone Mild

Ornamental entertainment or partners in wildness?

'We continually malign the good girl as "repressed", while the bad girl is (wrongly) perceived as intrinsically expressing her individuality and somehow proving her sexuality.' So says Wendy Shalit in her 2007 book *Girls Gone Mild*. If the book had been published a decade earlier she may have had a point, but the idea that the so-called 'bad girl' is expressing anything except silliness, weakness and capitulation to the forces of a patriarchal capitalist society is today rather quaint.

In her *Female Chauvinist Pigs* Ariel Levy gives a name—'raunch culture'—to the phenomenon of accessories and attitudes from the sex industry (*Pornstar* T-shirts, spangled G-strings, pole-dancing classes,

Brazilian waxes) that infiltrate mainstream culture. Published in 2005, Levy's thesis is that the language of feminism has been misused to defend and encourage a misogynous model of female sexuality. The result, according to Levy, is a culture in which women express their sexuality by 'acting like a cartoon woman, who has big cartoon breasts, wears little cartoon outfits and can only express her sexuality by spinning around a pole'.

The central concern of Levy's book (and the discussion it spawned) is not the sex industry itself but the mainstream adoption of its aesthetics and values. Women working as strippers or prostitutes are understood to be playing a role, but women who emulate sex workers are, according to Levy, playing the role of someone playing a role. Raunch isn't an expression of sexuality at all, only another performance. And, as evident from the title of Levy's book, women are to blame because we have apparently decided to beat the Male Chauvinist Pigs at their own game, not by turning the objectifying gaze back on them, but by objectifying ourselves.

Pamela Paul's 2006 book, *Pornified*, expressed a similar concern with the sexualisation of society:

> The all-pornography, all-the-time mentality is everywhere in today's pornified culture…It's on *Maxim* magazine covers where even women who ostensibly want to be taken seriously as actresses pose like *Penthouse* pinups. It's in women's magazines where readers are urged to model themselves on strippers, articles explain how to work your sex moves after those displayed in pornos and columnists counsel bored or dissatisfied young women to rent pornographic films with their lovers in order to 'enliven' their sex lives…

It's hard to disagree with much of what Paul and Levy say. Popular culture *is* dominated by images that used to be found only in porn magazines. Words like 'empowerment' and 'liberation' are being misused to advertise Brazilian waxes and breast implants. Women are often presented, in Levy's words, as 'ornamental entertainment' rather than 'partners in wildness'.

The 2007 American Psychological Association (APA) *Report of the Task Force on the Sexualization of Girls*, which drew together existing research on the extent and effects of sexualised images of women, seemed to supply the data to back up Levy's and Paul's anecdotal evidence. The report concluded that 'throughout US culture, and particularly in mainstream media, women and girls are depicted in a sexualising manner', and that the 'sexualisation [of girls] has negative effects in a variety of domains, including cognitive functioning, physical and mental health, and healthy sexual development'.

And yet we don't have the whole story. The APA report was based on a large, disparate group of studies, none of which in fact showed a causal link between sexualised images and poor mental or physical health outcomes. So, while there is documentary evidence that female models are photographed in sexualised positions more often than male models, and there are studies revealing that girls with high-level exposure to media have low self-esteem, there isn't much to prove that it's the sexiness of the models that is causing the problems, or whether all girls are susceptible, or if there are other factors at work. As the report's authors acknowledge, 'research documenting the pervasiveness and influence of such products and portrayals is sorely needed'. More research is especially needed to test the effects of sexualised media on girls, as opposed to women, on whom most existing research has been conducted.

Of course, you'd only know this if you read past the press release, which many reporting on the APA paper clearly did not. I read hundreds of newspaper and magazine articles that either cited or focused on the report and the vast majority of them jumped straight to the easy, sensationalist line: girls today are far too sexualised.

Little tarts vs. baby brides

'I want my little girls to look like little girls. I don't want them to look like little tarts,' wrote a commentator in the *Scotsman*. This sounds reasonable but begs the question. What *should* a little girl look like? Sugar and spice and all things nice? Yes, according to a *Herald Sun* editorial protesting pop star Kylie Minogue's range of tweeny underwear. 'Little girls,' it declared, 'should dress up like princesses, not down like sex kittens…'

If I was Queen of the World, all kids clothing would be designed for maximum play-ability and no parent would consider for a second putting their child in something that wasn't comfortable and suitable for tree-climbing, water-fighting, bike-riding or whatever activity the day demands. Except of course for dress-up time when kids would be free to put on any ridiculous, impractical costume their enchanting little brains could imagine. But for those who love the idea of fantasy clothing for kids, is there really much difference between a halter top (sexy) and a white-lacy frock (bridal)?

I don't think so. Both 'raunchy' clothes and the frilly dresses of my childhood emphasise gender; both are designed to make little girls conform to a particular image: trendy on the one hand, girlish on the other. For all the fuss about Bratz dolls and toddler-sized bras, I haven't seen any evidence that clothes and toys promoting beauty and fashion are any more oppressive to little girls than the tiny aprons, tea-sets and ironing boards of my childhood.

This is not to say I think G-strings for five-year-olds aren't disturbing, only that the real issue—inappropriate premature sexualisation—is distorted when we focus on appearances. In the 2006 film *Little Miss Sunshine*, eight-year-old Olive dreams of winning a beauty pageant. She's a cute, normal-looking girl with long brown hair, big eyes behind big glasses, short legs and a pot belly. The other contestants—all JonBenet Ramsey clones—perform routines straight off MTV, full of serious, come-hither facial expressions and slow, sexy moves. Olive's routine, taught to her by her larrikin grandpa, is a classic striptease. Although her shirt and shorts remain on, the rest is pure Showgirls: she crawls on all fours and growls at the audience, thrusts her hips and rubs her backside with a scarf. But, throughout, her face is open and glowing with joy and fun. There's nothing sexy about her stripper moves because she doesn't know that's what they are.

What's hard to describe but is absolutely apparent on film is how perfectly shocking *and* perfectly innocent Olive's performance is. Her failure to attempt to disguise the sexual content she doesn't understand contrasts with the too-adult awareness evident in the other girls' performance. It is clear that skimpy clothes or hip-shaking dance moves do not sexualise these kids. Not, that is, without the adults who teach them the way a fully sexual adult might wear the clothes or make the moves.

Little Miss Sunshine was released in Australia in October 2006, the same month that the Australia Institute's (AI) provocatively titled discussion paper 'Corporate Paedophilia' was published. The paper accused kidswear retailers of using sexualised images of children to sell their products and suggested that exposure to advertising, magazines and music videos prematurely sexualises girls.

Looking at the images used in the AI report as examples of 'sexualisation', I did feel disturbed. Not by the pictures which were all of cute kids wearing cute clothes, but by the idea that some adults described the pictures as 'sexy'. A few of the child models look awkward as they strike poses similar to those struck by adult models (hands on hip, head tilted, ultra serious expression) and a few are wearing heavy make-up, but there is no evidence of sexual awareness in any of the photos, no sign—to my eye—that the models are anything other than normal kids dressed up in special clothes, posing for the camera.

My initial reaction (and that of several other commentators) was that since there was nothing wrong with the pictures, there must be something wrong with the authors' perceptions. Why, I wondered, did they find pictures of children sexy? But then I picked up a copy of the tweeny targeted *Total Girl* magazine and realised that the issue was far more complicated.

The AI report claimed that 'over half' of *Total Girl*'s content was 'sexualising material', but on my cover to cover reading I saw not even a hint of sexuality. What I did see was a preoccupation with appearance: step-by-step instructions on how to create various hairstyles, several fashion spreads, commentary from celebrities about how they put together their 'look', advertorials for software that allows you to scan photos of yourself into a computer and try out different hair and make-up styles.

And it clicked: the authors of the AI report read this content so differently from the way I did, not because they saw the kids as sexy but because they see female beauty culture itself as sexual. If women wear make-up and follow fashion trends because they want to be sexually attractive, then pictures of girls made-up and coiffed according to adult instructions is a form of sexualisation.

And, well, it is and it isn't. Some of the pampering and primping that teenagers and adult women do is undoubtedly motivated by a desire to be 'sexy', but much of it is about fitting in, one way or another. For pre-pubescent girls, it's a matter of imitating older girls and is as indicative of future behaviour as is 'nursing' baby-dolls. So while a twenty-five-year-old or a fifteen-year-old may or may not be wearing lipstick in order to attract sexual partners, the ten-year-old and five-year-old are most certainly not.

And even if we talk solely about older teenagers and young adults—sexually mature people making decisions in a non-parentally supervised context—most reportage of this issue seems to express a form of moral panic. Typical is a *Sun-Herald* feature article on the 'new girl power' that name-checks Paris Hilton and Britney Spears before jumping to the conclusion that 'teenage girls and women in their 20s think nothing of flashing their breasts and baring their bums'. The evidence given for this extraordinary claim is that 'shopping malls on a weekend or afternoon look like lap-dancing clubs'.

I'm not cheerleading for the marketers trying to convince thirteen-year-olds they must wear black lace panties to fit in, nor am I defending those who would tell girls that the most 'empowering' thing they can do is get their gear off for a drunken mob. I'm pointing out that it is possible to observe certain truths about popular culture, without leaping to conclude that every individual who takes on elements of that culture is a foolish slave to capitalism, fashion or anything else.

Raunch culture may be harmful. That doesn't mean every girl who appears to conform to it is damaged beyond repair. Not every young woman who takes pole-dancing classes or wears a tight T-shirt is a helpless dupe of patriarchal desires. The relationship of an individual to her cultural environment is surely more complicated than that, and the debates we have need to embrace these complications.

The meaning of a miniskirt

A good friend of mine was told by a senior co-worker that she should 'rethink her clothing'. She asked for clarification. 'You tend to dress like a slut,' she was told. Note the accusation was not that she *was* a slut, but that she dressed like one.

If we agree that the term *slut* means to have more sexual partners than the user of the term finds acceptable, what does it mean to dress like one? Amongst the women I know there is absolutely no way you could guess who has slept with the most men simply by looking. Hell, look at me in my baggy jeans and overcoat, and try to guess my sexual history by the way I dress.

Back to my friend who was told she dressed like a slut at work. I started to describe what she was wearing when this comment was made, but I deleted it. Because, however much I want to defend her by explaining why her outfit wasn't 'slutty', doing so would imply that, had it been skimpier/shorter/tighter/different, then she would have deserved the label.

I know a woman who had the phrase 'Muslim bitch' thrown at her as she passed a group of young men outside a convenience store. Her reaction, and that of all of us who heard about the verbal attack, was to label those young men ignorant, bigoted pigs. The idea that she somehow brought this on herself because of her clothing is frankly offensive.

Yet my 'slutty' friend looked immediately to herself to discover why she had been insulted, and almost everyone she told about the incident asked her to describe what she was wearing at the time, as though the answer would somehow excuse or explain the insult. Why do women, who would not dream of blaming the victim of racial or religious vilification, automatically move to check what they might have done to 'incite' sexist insults?

The comparison with my hijab-wearing friend is apt. Some people would argue that she did indeed incite the thugs by dressing in a way that advertises her faith. As this well rehearsed argument goes, women who wear the hijab know that they stand out in the community and so can't complain when they are abused or discriminated against because they are choosing to draw attention to themselves.

There are plenty of problems with this line of argument, but two in particular are relevant to the discussion about my allegedly slutty-clothed friend. First is the assumption that women's clothing is a costume meant to signify to our audience what role we are playing, and that we should not complain when our audience responds accordingly.

Of course clothing is a social signal. Many people dress to signal their rejection of mainstream aesthetics or their identification with a sub-culture, for example. Adherents of certain religious groups do the same thing. Even those of us who don't dress to express membership of a specific group, do adjust our attire depending on the location. We do this because we understand that jeans and sneakers 'say' something different from a suit or a bikini or a cocktail dress.

But recognising that clothing is a social signifier is not the same as saying that it invites a specific response. You see a woman in a dress that reveals a lot of skin: maybe her choice of clothing signifies a desire for attention. Maybe it signifies that she is part of mainstream fashion culture. Maybe she loves the colour or fabric. Maybe she wants to keep cool while out dancing. It's not the right of others to pass judgment on what a woman is 'saying' or 'asking for' by dressing in a particular way.

The other problem with assuming that women in hijab or short skirts or whatever are inviting a particular kind of attention is that it's impossible to anticipate how a random person will react. You might think your mid-calf skirt and long-sleeve blouse is modest but that Taliban wannabe at the bus stop could become inflamed by your naked ankles. And the woman who was abused for wearing a hijab may leave it off next time and be insulted instead for her form-fitting skirt.

Certain ways of dressing may attract more attention than others, but some men will continue to insult women on the street no matter what the women are wearing. The office creep who stares at his colleague's breasts or legs will do so regardless of how she is dressed, and there has probably never been a rapist who has let a potential victim walk on by because her dress was ankle length.

The subject of slutty clothing becomes particularly fraught when it is concentrated on teenagers. I don't know how many times I've heard men—nice, progressive, liberal men—make comments along the lines of 'I wouldn't let my daughter dress like [Paris Hilton/catwalk model/any girl standing at a bus stop] because I know how teenage boys think'. It's not sexist to suggest teenage girls cover up, they argue, because it's a biological fact that teenage boys are obsessed with sex and will think about, if not try to initiate, intimate acts with said innocent but skimpily dressed young girls.

Let's get real: teenage girls do sometimes wear skimpy clothes. Teen midriffs are exposed; barely formed breasts are revealed in T-shirts; adolescent thighs are on display even in the dead of winter. So, there is some truth in claims that gals today dress like hookers. You know who else they dress like? Their mothers. I've seen photos of my mum and her sisters as teenagers and they're wearing skirts so short that I'm sure someone wrote an editorial about the improper influence of Twiggy.

The clothing of 'young people today' is exactly the same as the clothing of young people yesterday (every yesterday) in that it is designed to: a) differentiate their generation from the one previous—whether Mum is a right-on feminist or a traditional homemaker, dressing like a burlesque dancer will work nicely to show the world you are *not* your mother; b) identify with a culture or sub-culture; and c) display sexual awareness and interest.

Obviously it's the last one that agitates parents and excites the commentariat into a scarcely concealed sexual hypocrisy. The Australian current affairs magazine the *Monthly* illustrated an article about 'sex and power in the age of pornography' with a full-page photo of teenage girls in very short skirts. The *Sun-Herald*'s feature titled 'Sass to sleaze:

the new girl power', worried that raunch culture has 'gone too far' and then went rather far itself using three close-up photos of starlets' breasts, another pic of a singer's bare thighs and one of a pole dancer. The presentation of these two articles is representative of the mainstream media's approach to the subject: young women are perved on, photographed, used to sell papers and then told to stop being so damn sexual.

But teenagers, whatever they wear, *are* sexual. We seem to have no trouble accepting this about boys: think of modern pop culture classics like *American Pie* or *Road Trip* in which the quest for sex is an integral part of male bonding and coming of age. The fact that male sexuality is not feared and restricted like female sexuality is evident in the way our culture looks at teenagers. Adults may roll their eyes at boys with their pants half fallen down but there's no panic about boys showing their bums in order to attract sexual partners.

Yes, clothes for teen girls do tend to reveal more flesh than those for boys, but that's a reflection of a culture in which (perhaps with the exception of wedding dresses) women are usually provided with less fabric than men (think tux compared to evening gown; men's business shirt compared to women's), rather than a signal that they're up for an orgy. They may well be up for that or anything else, of course, but their outfits aren't going to tell you that. Clothes do communicate messages, but you have to understand the language to read them properly and, when it comes to teen culture, most adults don't have a clue.

Teenage boys, on the other hand, do. Many of them are also, it is fair to say, preoccupied with sex, but that fact has no connection to what the girls around them are wearing. A heterosexual teenage boy is capable of being turned on by anything even resembling a woman's body. If a girl goes to school in a shapeless sack, teenage boys will spend all day imagining what is under it. Does anyone think boys in the 1950s didn't have fantasies about what the girls hid underneath their pleated skirts?

The meaning of covering up

American writer Wendy Shalit is a sort of mother hen of the so-called 'modesty movement', which has emerged over the last decade in reaction to the alleged 'pornification' of our culture. Shalit's books, *A Return to Modesty* (1999) and *Girls Gone Mild* (2007), argue that women were better off before the sexual revolution and that the only way to halt the epidemics of anorexia, drug abuse and self-mutilation amongst young women is to promote chastity. Shalit also founded the Modesty Zone website and is a frequent contributor to the Modestly Yours blog, a forum in which twenty-one young women write about the challenges and rewards of living the modest life.

Arguing for a return to long skirts, lowered eyelashes and premarital abstinence, Shalit writes in *A Return to Modesty* that 'without modesty, we are lost—not excited by anything much, and not knowing what the problem is...maybe we're not having fun because everything is permitted. Maybe without modesty, we forget what is erotic'.

It's an interesting, if not original, argument. As any striptease artist knows, it's what's not yet revealed that is exciting; as soon as one part of the body is uncovered the punters begin salivating over what remains hidden. But acknowledging the erotic possibilities of dressing to conceal is not the same as proclaiming that women should keep themselves covered to ensure their future husbands find them sexy. Men get turned on by girls who've stayed chaste, Shalit writes. 'Modesty is proof that morality is sexy.' When said in this context, 'cover yourself up' is as degrading as 'show us yer tits'. In each case a woman's body is something to be displayed or hidden according to how horny it makes a man.

Modesty advocates assume that women's dress choices are all about men and their anticipated reactions, but what if the woman wearing tiny shorts is a size 16? Is she emulating a pornstar in order to attract male attention? What about a post-menopausal woman with stretch marks wearing a bikini—is she advertising her availability?

Women who are not young/thin/firm/big-breasted, and who choose fitted or skimpy clothing often provoke scorn and cries of 'cover up' or 'wear something more appropriate'. But if they hide their non-approved bodies, are they not pandering to the patriarchal gaze as much as the slim young things who squeeze into tube tops and micro-minis? A friend explained why she wears long pants even on the hottest summer days: 'I'm cursed with sensitive skin and super-thick, fast-growing body hair. If I shave my legs every day I get a painful rash, but if I skip a day I have thick black stubble. So I'm stuck with long pants if I don't want men to think I'm gross.'

The argument that bare-skin equals sexy shows a lack of imagination and understanding about the relationship between what pop culture says is erotic and what individuals experience as being erotic. Modesty advocates have accepted raunch culture's assertion that bare flesh equals sex and bare female flesh equates to a sexual invitation. They're buying exactly what mass culture is selling them.

As with raunch culture's sexy imperative, the modesty message is directed exclusively towards women. We should dress modestly because it helps boys control themselves or makes our husbands horny. We should look at our bodies as sites of shame and sin and sex. We should look at ourselves the way a lustful stranger on the street would do. We should think of ourselves as performers, inciters, controllers, seducers, but never human beings going about our daily lives, wearing clothes we like.

Raunch culture and the modesty movement are two sides of the same coin. Both see women primarily in terms of their attractiveness and availability. Both are ultimately conservative worldviews: they not only cast women as objects of men's gaze and judgment, they also assume that women should care what that judgment is, and dress and act accordingly.

How to treat girls as people

In *Girls Gone Mild*, Shalit talks about the choice 'between emotional repression and sexual repression', arguing that the latter is better than the former but missing the fact that many people manage to choose neither. She also leaves out all those for whom sexual repression would cause or constitute emotional repression and vice versa. Similarly, while Ariel Levy is right to say that 'raunchy and liberated are not synonyms', it's important to acknowledge that they're not antonyms either.

As a teenager I remember overhearing a comment from a friend. 'Emily,' she said, with a tone of withering pity she usually reserved for housewives and veiled women, 'just wants boys to like her'. Her words were true—I *did* want boys to like me—but her tone skewered me. The implication was that I wanted boys to like me because I was missing something within myself. I was insecure or needy or desperate. I accepted that this was probably true and added *you just want boys to like you* to my mental loop of self-criticism.

What I wish I'd been able to figure out at the time was that wanting boys to like me was okay. I was a hormone-fuelled heterosexual teenage girl—having boys like me was central to my desires. I didn't particularly care if boys fell in love with me or wanted to be my best friend; as long as the ones I liked enough to want to get snugly with liked me enough to want the same thing, then I was happy. My brashness was designed to attract male attention, but that doesn't mean it wasn't an authentic expression of my sexuality. To have sat in the corner waiting for a boy to speak to me (let alone get naked with me) would have been a denial of self.

This is why the critics of showy young women run the risk of reinforcing the old stereotype about women being not as sexually interested or expressive as men. If we say that the sexually expressive woman is only playing up to men's desires, then we deny that women have desires and expressions of their own, and that sometimes these coincide with mainstream versions of sexuality.

Equally, though, we can't ignore the fact that some young women feel pressured to exhibit their sexuality in a mainstream way. Annie Bennett is the bright, confident twenty-something spokesperson for the Australian Christian abstinence campaign group Worth the Wait. I asked her how she—a woman who chooses not to be sexually active—feels about sexuality in the media.

> The media portrays an image of sex that just isn't realistic. Magazines educate girls, some not even teenagers, about the best sexual positions, which suggests to me that everyone is doing it and that we all have to be experts. It's just not the truth. This pressure to conform impacts self respect, self esteem, image...The media pushes that you have to look a certain way to get a guy to love you to be worth anything. The pressure is to perform sexually, look good, etc. The media promotes that everyone is doing it and that we all have to be super thin sex gods, which is so not true...

I hate that some girls feel pressured to be sexual in a particular, male-centred, media-driven way. I hate that girls don't feel free to explore their sexuality in their own way, at their own pace, without the world looking on and passing judgment. I hate that there are adults who feel entitled to demand certain sexual behaviours from teenagers, and I hate that there are adults who think it is okay to exploit girls in order to sell their products and promote their brands.

But, rather than moving back and forth from one narrow definition of sexual expression to another, we should be trying to broaden the possibilities. Most people will go through several phases in their sexual lives: romantic crushes at school, messing around and making mistakes at university, an extended period of monogamy, abstinence while recovering from a broken heart, cautious semi-casual sex while re-entering the dating world, monogamy again, and so on. The 'slut', the 'virgin', the 'girl gone wild' and the sexually conservative mother of three are likely to be all the same person.

The question must be, then, how do we encourage girls and women to experience and express their sexuality authentically or even to figure out what authentic sexuality is amongst all this background noise telling them what it should be? Well, maybe we can't. Maybe there's no such thing as authentic sexuality. Nevertheless, I'm confident we can do better than we are currently doing.

The first step must be comprehensive sex education that is free of gender bias and biological determinism, that has an emphasis on respect and consent, and that teaches young people that sexual urges are natural and healthy.

Outside of schools, those who care about the self-esteem and well-being of young people need to change the way they talk about women's bodies and sexual choices. In article after article in major newspapers from around the world, teenage girls and young women are referred to in terms that reinforce tired, damaging stereotypes. Either they're fragile and in need of protection or they're wild and slutty. They're princesses or pornstars.

Even those who should know better, such as Australian psychologist Michael Carr-Gregg, talk about girls as if their bodies are troublesome objects that must be controlled. Carr-Gregg told the *Weekend Australian Magazine* that pubescent girls 'look like they're ready for everything but they don't really know anything at all. It's like having this beautiful, sleek vehicle but the driver isn't licensed'. Carr-Gregg is describing what he thinks about girls' bodies; he's not saying anything at all about what it may be like to be an adolescent girl. I guarantee that no adolescent girl has *ever* felt she 'has' a sleek vehicle; I bet almost every girl (every boy, too) feels she or he is a person going through a tumultuous, confusing time of life.

And a girl never has to learn to 'drive' her body—a body is not something separate from the human being living in it. Yes, girls (and boys) must learn to take care of their adult bodies (that's where the sex education comes in), but so too must we all learn to deal with adult relationships and the emotions that come with them. Funny how nobody talks about girls' maturing intellects as separate pieces of machinery for use of which they must gain a permit.

That someone who works with adolescent girls could use such an inappropriate metaphor tells us a lot about how even some experts continue to view female bodies as threatening, sinister objects that must be kept under surveillance for the wellbeing and safety of the community.

Those who worry that girls are being ruined or damaged by their desire for equality and liberation demonstrate good old-fashioned sexism dressed up as social concern. They should remember how people once fretted that, if girls received the same education as boys, their ovaries would shrivel up. Later, some feared that female suffrage would 'lower' women and disrupt the social fabric. Very recently, we have heard that women who work outside the home are responsible for destroying families. And now we're supposed to panic about the danger of telling girls they are in control of their own bodies.

Instead of criticising young women for not dressing or acting 'correctly' we need to work on creating a culture in which women are not judged on the length of their skirt or the size of their breasts, in which they are safe from sexual harassment and violence, regardless of what they have chosen to wear, and in which their sexual expression is understood separately from the desires of men.

4
Defensive Sex Education

Curiosity and ignorance

When I was fourteen, I wanted to have sex more than I wanted anything else in the world. Let me be clear: I did not want to have sex because the media told me I should or because my friends were doing it or my boyfriend was pushing me. I wanted to have sex because my body was flooded with hormones whose entire reason for existence was to make me want to have sex.

I was so desperate for assurance that my desire was normal and didn't mean I was destined to be pregnant at sixteen and dying of AIDS by twenty, that I put my faith in a Year 9 Health and Development class at my school. I was disappointed. Female sexual development, according to my teacher, was an embarrassing, uncomfortable process, but it would allow me one day to experience the miracle of motherhood. I learnt about ovulation and menstruation. I learnt that the appearance of pubic hair on a girl signals an increase in androgen levels, and that tender breasts and swollen nipples indicate a rise in estrogen. I also learnt that testosterone was surging through my body and might cause me to feel 'strange'.

Boys would not feel 'strange': they would feel horny. They would be distracted by sexual thoughts and feelings. Their genitals would engorge with blood for no reason at all. They would feel a deep, low ache which could only be eased by sexual release. They would have erotic dreams from which they would wake to find they had messed up their sheets and pyjamas. *I am a boy*, I thought, my face hot and my thighs pressed together.

Girls in many classrooms today still feel the same mix of curiosity, bewilderment and shame. Although all secondary schools in the UK and Australia, for instance, are required to include sex education in the curriculum, the specific content and nature of the lessons is up to individual schools, and many decide to stick to basic biology. Non-government schools often supplement the scientific and medical information with lessons in morals or values according to their particular religious traditions, and some state schools add lessons in sexual stereotyping and assertiveness.

It's evidently not enough. A recent study by the University of Southampton, for the UK sexual health charity Brook, found that only a third of sexually active teenagers use condoms regularly, and about half don't know how emergency contraception works. More than half think only women get chlamydia, and a quarter don't know that sexually transmitted infections (STIs) can be transmitted via oral sex. The consequences of this ignorance are grave: STIs are on the increase amongst UK teenagers.

In Australia, a 2002 study by La Trobe University found that more than 10 percent of students in Years 10 and 12 did not know that HIV can be transmitted during sex between men. Almost a quarter did not know that HIV can be spread from a pregnant woman to her baby *in utero* and more than 15 percent did not know that 'someone who looks healthy' could pass on an HIV infection. Such ignorance no doubt contributes to the relaxed attitude teens have to safe sex precautions. Only 65.8 percent of the sexually active teens in Year 10 and only 51.8 percent of those in Year 12 always used a condom. As the researchers concluded, 'knowledge is not, in and of itself, a means of STI prevention, [but] it is a necessary precursor of safe behaviour'.

In the US, where the federal government provides financial incentives to schools that have abstinence-only sex education, the situation is even more dire. The government's support means that not only do many schools adopt such programs out of economic pragmatism, but that the sometimes inaccurate, alarmist information supplied by abstinence educators is given official credibility. The website of the Louisiana Governor's Program for Abstinence, warns, for example, that 'cancer, infertility, death...are the possible consequences of having sex'. And don't even think about relying on condoms, because, according to the Ohio-based Abstinence Educators' Network, 'disease particles are a lot smaller than sperm, which is what condoms were invented to stop'. There are no studies cited to back up these frightening 'facts'.

These examples are not exceptional: a US Congress analysis in 2004 of abstinence-only education found that such programs 'frequently [provide] inaccurate or misleading information, often in direct contradiction to the findings of government scientists'.

What does it matter if the facts are exaggerated and unsubstantiated, some may ask, as long as it stops teenagers from becoming statistics of disease and early pregnancy. If only it worked like that. Multiple US studies have shown that while abstinence-only education does not reduce the likelihood of teenagers having pre-marital sex, it *does* reduce the likelihood of teens practising safe sex.

But even seemingly comprehensive sex education programs often leave young people unprepared. I met Sarah Hunt, a twenty-year-old Sydney university student, at a women's health conference where she was the only non-professional on a panel about sex education. While the other speakers discussed what makes for good sex education, Sarah spoke about receiving the kind of sex education most progressives think of as 'good' but which turned out to be almost useless.

'I went to a big co-ed school in a country town,' she said. 'I remember lots of really frank discussion about contraception and where babies come from and how condoms protect you from STIs. There was even some nice talk about relationships and not letting yourself be pressured into sex and I'm sure the school thought they were being progressive and doing a really good job.'

But, said Sarah, 'the first time I had sex—and all the other times after that, actually—there were no condoms involved, there was no contraception involved. There were, in fact, no penises involved. So the sex education I got was, in fact, totally worthless to me. In those classes at school it was barely acknowledged that two women could have sex together, let alone how they should protect themselves when they do it.'

Through 'books, the internet and asking embarrassing questions' Sarah discovered which STIs can be transmitted through what sexual contact, what precautions were available to protect against them and how to negotiate these issues with the women she had sex with. For gay and lesbian students like Sarah, lessons on how not to get pregnant are far from adequate.

Real-life sex encompasses much more than the penetration of a woman by a man for the purpose of procreation, and this is especially true for teenagers who engage in a far wider range of sexual experimentation than most adults. Not for them three minutes of kissing followed by safe and efficient grown-up intercourse. Teen sexual activity is about hands and mouths as much as it is about genitals. It is about curiosity as much as satisfaction, about figuring out what feels good and what doesn't, what you want and what you don't.

Teenagers are not doing all this adventurous touching because the media is saturated with sexual images or because they lack moral guidance; they're doing it because they are sexual beings. We can tell them to 'just say no' and we can refuse to provide information about sex, but we cannot take their sexuality away. It is part of them and it will be expressed.

Dangerous silences

Back when I was a teen, the word was that only unloved girls with low self-esteem let boys use them for sex. And *using* it would be, because boys were only after one thing and, if you gave them that, you would never see them again. *Fine*, I thought, *let them use me. Bring it on*. But the teenage boys with one-track minds must have gone to a different school, and the men who coax innocent schoolgirls into bed must have done their seducing in another town. So I had to learn to 'be a man'—to do the seducing that nobody was doing to me. It was hard work and there was no way I'd risk blowing the whole deal right at the crucial moment by acting like a girl and talking about my feelings and concerns.

Looking back, I am horrified at the risks I took with my health and safety. My limited sex education, combined with the ridiculous gender stereotypes I'd absorbed, left me incredibly vulnerable. Of course I knew that I could get pregnant or worse, but I was so ashamed of my desire, and so grateful for whatever action I was getting, that the last thing on my mind was avoiding infection or insemination.

My experience cannot, of course, be extrapolated to every teenager, but it does, I believe, reveal the central problem with both official sex education programs and unofficial but socially sanctioned discourses about adolescent sexuality. Giving teenagers information about sex is pointless if you don't also teach them how to incorporate this information into their lives and self-image.

When a trio of eighteen-year-old girls I barely knew agreed to meet with me and talk frankly about their sexual activities, I was surprised but appreciative. I made it clear to them that I was recording their words, promised them anonymity and then, without my asking a question, they started talking.

They each had very specific lists of things they will and won't do with their boyfriends. They will, for example, 'pash' each other ('boys love it and we don't mind it so why not?'), talk dirty ('just porn stuff, you know, "ooh you're so big" or whatever') and perform a striptease ('it's like dancing, no biggie'). They are all apparently 'pros' at giving head and hand jobs. One of them lets her boyfriend 'tit fuck' her, which her friends think is 'repulsive'. None has had penetrative sex. Why? 'I think it should be saved for someone you really love,' says one girl. The others agree. 'Guys don't care that much about doing it, as long as you get them off somehow.' What about the girls though? Do their boyfriends get them off? They giggle, shrug, go quiet. 'It's not about that,' one says.

These girls knew almost everything there was to know about sex. They knew how to perform sex acts they've never done and say they don't plan to do. They knew where to get and how to use condoms, dental dams, lube and the morning-after pill. They comfortably use both the correct anatomical and crude slang terms for male and female genitals. But when it came to questions of their own sexual pleasure, they morphed into coy, 1950s wallflowers. 'That stuff's private,' one said, her friends nodding at the floor.

And it is, so I didn't push it. But the difference between how they talked about what they do, and didn't talk about what they enjoy, was striking. It reminded me of Year 9 Health and Development class: everybody was talking about anatomy, mechanics and safety; nobody was discussing the really important things.

Important questions like: how do I know whether this will feel good? What if I don't like it? What if the person I'm having sex with doesn't like having it with me? How do I say no to someone without hurting their feelings? How do I make a person stop doing something I don't want to do? How do I ask a person to do something I do want them to do? Does wanting [sexual fantasy of choice] make me [weird/bad/a freak/criminal/destined to be alone forever]? Am I [a freak/perverted/weird] for even thinking about this stuff? Is it okay to want to have sex with someone I don't like? Is it okay not to want to have sex with someone I do like?

And nobody—not my Health and Development teachers, not my school friends and not my three eighteen-year-old interviewees—*nobody* talks about female masturbation. When I called a couple of my most reliable female correspondents to canvass the issue, I was told I had gone one question too far. Remarkably, even a woman who happily talked to me about her consumption of porn made it clear that she used it only with partners, never alone.

Why the silence? It comes back to the idea that only men (and damaged women) want sex for its own sake. When a girl has sex it should be because she is in love, or at the very least, in the grip of a serious crush. Even having admitted I was desperate for sex as a teenager, I am reluctant to take the confession that one step further. It seems shameful to admit that my sexuality was *in* me rather than inspired by a particular boy (or boys).

But the truth is my teenage yearnings were remarkably unfocused and my understanding of how to deal with them was limited. When my first attempt at getting myself off failed, I assumed that the only solution was to find a partner to do it for me. It seems ludicrous that a girl of average intelligence could believe that a fumbling boy would know her body better than she did, but when the only sex education you've had consisted of lectures on puberty and intercourse, and your only idea about relationships comes from American movies, well, you end up with some strange ideas.

I'm not advocating for step-by-step instructions to be issued in schools, but an acknowledgment that masturbation is natural, healthy and completely safe would be helpful. Telling girls and boys that there are lots of ways to do it and that taking your time and experimenting is the only way to find what works for you would, I suspect, be as much instruction as most hormone-riddled teens need.

That female masturbation is still so taboo is a great shame, because it has loads of benefits, especially for adolescent girls. It allows sexual experimentation and release without the risk or compromise associated with a lot of teenage sex, and allows a girl to feel at ease with her own body and her sexual responses. Given that an estimated 70 percent of women cannot climax from vaginal penetration alone, being able to bring yourself to orgasm and to show a partner what gets you off, is an important relationship skill.

DIY sex ed

Like most girls of my generation, I relied heavily on *Dolly* magazines, then *Cleo*, to find answers to my questions about sex, and it would seem girls today are no different. A survey by UK *CosmoGIRL!* (average reader age fourteen) found that 76 percent of its readers feel happier turning to a magazine agony aunt for sexual health advice rather than their parents or a doctor. A 2007 report by UK education watchdog Ofsted backed up *CosmoGIRL!*'s finding, confirming that teen girls are more likely to get sex information from magazines than any other source.

The Ofsted report noted that women's glossies are a mixed bag when it comes to sex education for girls. 'While many magazines stress the importance of safe sex, some indicate inaccurately a perception that all young people are sexually active...On the other hand, the problem pages remain a positive source of advice and reassurance for many young people.'

Dolly magazine's 'Dolly Doctor' section was my Bible when I was fourteen. I picked up a copy of the magazine recently to see if it was as good as I remembered, and it was even better. In response to a girl worried about 'growths' on her vagina, 'Dolly Doctor' explains the changes female genitals go through during puberty, reassures the girl that she's probably perfectly fine but recommends a trip to the doctor and a chat to her mum just to be sure. A girl who'd been raped while drunk is given compassionate advice about dealing with psychological and emotional trauma and practical help with pregnancy and STI testing. This issue also had page-length articles on contraception, vaginal health and STI symptoms and treatment. *Dolly*'s main Australian competitor *Girlfriend* is just as impressive, with a five-page advice section giving sensible, practical, non-judgmental advice on everything from correct bra fitting to irregular periods, from unprotected intercourse to same-sex experimentation.

Of course, many young people read magazines produced for an adult audience and the messages about sex in these can be careless at best and misogynous at worst. This is particularly a problem for boys. There isn't a male equivalent of adolescent-friendly *Dolly*, so boys go straight from *KidsZone* to *Loaded*. 'Lads mags', as they're called in the UK, are sold as lifestyle rather than porn publications but their content is mostly sleaze and gore. *FHM*, for example, encourages readers to send in photos of breasts taken without the woman's knowledge. *Zoo* has a 'glamour model' as its sex advice columnist and recently ran a competition in which the winner received a new set of breasts for his girlfriend.

It's easy (though justifiable) to pick on lads mags, but all mainstream magazines, regardless of their target audience or advice columnists, contain a great deal of sexist advertising, images and messages. Most sex-related articles reinforce all those old ideas about women having sex to win love and men pretending love to get sex, about women being chased and men chasing, about men being constantly horny and women needing hours of foreplay and persuasion before they'll 'give it up'. The women's magazines publish article after article about how to please men while the men's mags publish article after article on how to get women to please them. Fashion shoots aimed at women show scantily clad, erotically posed female models...and so do those aimed at men.

And then there's the internet which is equal parts terrifying and thrilling for those of us who want to see more and more diverse information on sexuality. In an interview at feminist website *www.centerfornewwords.org*, Heather Corinna, the founder of sexuality site *Scarleteen.com*, warned against presuming 'that because the internet is so vast, that the sexual information we find on it is equally vast'. The web, Corinna points out, is 'coloured by the same biases we find anywhere else. Heterocentricity and gendernormativity loom large on the web, as does all of the gender bias, class oppressions, and long-standing myths that are part of a lot of sexual information, including much sexual research'.

The biggest concern in terms of sex self-educating online is the ubiquitous pornography. Porn is not a good way for beginners to learn about sex. An adult who has had real-life sexual experience may be able to put the on-screen antics into some kind of context, but someone who has not had sex, who may not have even seen a naked adult, will have a difficult time interpreting what they see. Experienced adults may see that something is a fantasy scenario while inexperienced teens may see the same things as an ideal reality.

Nevertheless, the internet can be a terrific resource for learning about sex. Sites such as *Scarleteen.com*, *Avert.org* and *gURL.com* take a positive, inclusive, safety-conscious approach to sex. Chat rooms, web forums and bulletin boards allow teenagers to discuss anonymously their sexual problems, questions, doubts and concerns. The best of these web forums are moderated (to eliminate voyeurs and trouble-makers) and include the voices of older or more experienced women. As Heather Corinna says, 'the web has provided…an ongoing, diverse conversation as well as a gigantic public library. There are an awful lot of people out there who have found support via the web that they wouldn't have been able to find otherwise'.

Such communities may be particularly important to same-sex attracted teenagers, many of whom, like Sarah Hunt, have to gather independently the information that the heterosexist education system neglects to provide. As well as safer-sex information, the internet can provide a badly needed sense of community and moral support. A La Trobe University study of 200 same-sex attracted young Australians, conducted in 2001, found that the majority used the internet 'as a critical source of support and affirmation, particularly in the coming out process'. The report concluded that despite the potential dangers of the web 'we need to think of the internet as an important resource for marginalised young people' for whom the 'real' world was often 'unsafe and inhospitable'.

Of course our goal should be to make the world a safer, more hospitable place for teenagers of all sexual orientations. A supportive online community is a great thing, but not all teenagers have reliable access to the internet, and what's the point if the participants are then persecuted or neglected in school or on the streets?

How positive sex education helps keep girls safe

From puberty onwards most girls are now taught how to stay 'safe'. In sex-ed class, magazine articles, email forwards, advice from friends and lectures from parents, we are told that we can avoid rape if we don't go out alone or get drunk, if we carry our car keys as a weapon, take self-defence classes, don't dress revealingly, don't lead boys on, don't talk to strangers and on and on. We get it. We live it. And we still get raped. Sober or drunk, at home or away, wearing short skirts or hijabs, by strangers or by acquaintances, women continue to be victims of rape.

Here's a radical suggestion: direct the rape prevention message to boys. Write emails and advice columns and school sex-ed curriculum that say: don't rape. Don't rape drunken girls, beautiful girls, girls you're in love with, girls who've had sex with you, solitary girls, sleeping girls, flirtatious girls, any girls. Just don't.

Of course not many boys will grow up to become rapists, but that's no reason not to direct the message to them. Not a single woman has caused her own rape, not ever, and yet girls are bombarded with advice that can do nothing except cause our would-be rapist to find a different victim.

Rape is a male crime. There are female rapists but they are so rare as to be statistically insignificant. Acknowledging this does not minimise the suffering of their victims, nor does it excuse the perpetrators. It does, however, stop us from pretending that rape is a gender-neutral crime and thus allows us to confront those responsible for the overwhelming majority of rapes.

There is a culture of acceptance about the rape of women by men. This becomes clear when we think about the way male-to-male rape is perceived. Male-to-male rape is an horrific crime, but the victims are never blamed for putting themselves in harm's way by getting drunk or walking down a street alone. Men are not constantly lectured on how to behave so as not to attract rapists.

Consider why rape is thought to be more serious if the victim is a straight man or a female virgin. Do we think that a woman who has sex with men willingly in other circumstances shouldn't be so upset at having sex unwillingly? The huge misconception here is that rape is simply a rougher form of sex. It isn't. Rape is to sex what being beaten unconscious is to falling asleep. It is an act of violence visited upon a person's body and it is always traumatic.

This same misconception about rape-as-sex is evident in discussions over consent. Rape, by definition, cannot be committed with the victim's consent, yet this question comes up again and again. When a woman is raped she must prove she has not consented. What did she do to stop her attacker? Did she fight hard enough, say no often enough, scream loud enough? Wasn't she dressed as if she wanted to be penetrated? Didn't her drunkenness indicate she was up for anything? The answers to these questions are often used in lieu of evidence, to determine that an alleged rape was nothing more than a big misunderstanding. If only she had been clearer about not wanting to be raped!

Am I arguing that girls and women shouldn't be held responsible for their behaviour? Not at all. If a woman drinks to excess, then falls over in the street, loses her wallet and vomits all over her shirt, she has only herself to blame. But rape is not a consequence of getting drunk. It's a consequence of a man deciding to rape someone. Likewise, if a woman commits a crime while drunk—driving a car or beating someone up, say—she is responsible. But being raped is not a crime; raping someone is. In no other situation do we hear the victim being told to take responsibility for the criminal's actions.

Rape may seem an odd topic to discuss in the context of sex education but that's because we still consider rape to be something done by wicked strangers in dark alleys. In fact, more than 70 percent of sexual assaults are committed by someone known to the victim. Very often the rapist is a young man who doesn't understand that what he is doing is a crime or even wrong. In many cases, the assault is not reported for the same reason: the girl will blame herself for somehow not making her distress clear.

The worst sexual experiences I had as a teenager were those in which I and/or my partner had no idea how to communicate our discomfort with what was going on. From talking to other women and men I know my experiences were not unusual. The bad sex which turns into rape commonly goes like this: everything is going nicely, then at some point the physical tangling becomes less smooth. She may put up slight physical resistance—stiffening of limbs or not returning kisses, for example—but the lack of response is read as a call to do more, rather than to pull back. There may be tears or small pained noises. There's probably no firm 'stop' and so he doesn't, and when she breaks down or doesn't ever speak to him again he doesn't really know what went wrong, or when, or how.

Obviously we can't expect teenagers to be able to have sophisticated, articulate exchanges about sex (how many adults do?), but we can teach them to pay attention to body language and to check in with each other using simple monosyllables like 'OK?', 'yes', 'no', 'stop' and 'wait'. It would be helpful for girls and boys to understand that having said yes to someone or something in the past doesn't mean they have to say yes to everyone and everything.

Boys and girls also need to understand that pain, discomfort or reluctance are *not* normal female responses to sexual activity in which they have willingly engaged. I know I am not the only girl to have had a boy ignore or discount my objections, not out of cruelty or brutality, but because he believed that protesting is what girls do. I've no doubt there are many girls who believe this too. Which only adds to an already dangerous social environment. How can a girl complain about something that feels wrong if she believes sex should feel bad? Why wouldn't a boy pressure a girl for sex if he believes that is how it happens?

Our culture teaches boys that sex is something men must procure. The idea of coercion as foreplay is reinforced by jokes about plying girls with alcohol, stories about 'accidentally' running out of petrol while driving a girl home and shared strategising about how to 'convince' girls to have sex. It's easy to see how the line between convincing and forcing can become blurred for adolescent boys—and it does.

Sexuality researcher Doreen Rosenthal told the *Age* on 26 March 2007 that 'we know from research that some boys are deliberately getting girls drunk or stoned because they want to have sex with them. And there's another group of boys who may be pressuring girls generally to have sex, because they lack the knowledge about how to communicate with girls about sex'. Now, I don't believe for one second that these boys are sex-crazed beasts who willingly hurt girls or callously disregard their feelings. But when you combine a sexist culture with an inadequate education system, you get boys, who would no doubt condemn 'real rapists', telling researchers that it is acceptable to 'hold a girl down and force her to have sexual intercourse in instances such as when she gets him sexually excited or changes her mind'. According to a 2001 report in the *Journal of Interpersonal Violence*, 54 percent of teenage boys agreed with this comment.

Some abstinence-only education programs encourage the idea that there's something wrong with a girl who 'gives it up'. One such program operating in Seattle public schools, for example, asks students to consider why a girl who 'French kiss[es] on a first date' might be 'vulnerable to date rape'. But even relatively progressive sex education programs often reinforce the message that female sexuality is passive and male sexuality is aggressive. Lessons on consent, for example, are often based on the premise that boys pursue sex and girls delay or resist. Such a model sets up sexually confident or assertive girls as 'weird' or 'slutty' and, equally, it condemns sexually hesitant boys as weak or effeminate.

So, from the outset, we have a large number of people feeling that, in order to conform, they must behave in a way that might be contrary to their instincts. And we have a lot of teenagers expecting that people of the opposite sex will behave in a certain way. This can result in name-calling, bad reputations and sexual dissatisfaction, and eventually can contribute to the incidence of sexual assault.

It's right and necessary to worry about girls becoming victims of sexual assault; it's a shockingly common crime, but we will be better off changing the way we talk about sex to young men than issuing constant warnings to girls about how they should protect themselves.

Sex ed that shines

So what would a comprehensive sex education program look like? I discovered a terrific example in South Australia where the appropriately named SHine (Sexual Health Information, Networking and Education), a government-funded, administratively independent sexual health agency, ran a three-year pilot 'best practice' program in fifteen South Australian schools. SHine's Sexual Health and Relationships Education program was based on the understanding that sex education should be part of a 'lifelong process of acquiring information and forming values, beliefs and attitudes about identity, relationships, and intimacy'. According to the factors of success identified in a number of Australian and international studies, the program took a 'comprehensive, positive, interactive approach which acknowledged students as sexual beings with specific social and cultural identities, and one which addressed issues of gender and the meanings young men and women attribute to sexuality and sexual behaviour'.

What this means, in real terms, is that as well as the usual lessons on puberty, reproduction and STIs, the curriculum included lessons on body image, the social construction of gender, the influence of drugs on sexual decision-making and how to negotiate for safe sex. The program also taught students how to find, and assess the quality of, sexual health information on the internet.

SHine's inclusion of lessons on masturbation and sexual diversity provoked an outcry from some segments of the community that labelled it 'government-sponsored child abuse'.

Fortunately, support for SHine far outweighed the opposition and it received favourable independent assessments from La Trobe University and the University of South Australia, as well as overwhelmingly positive feedback from the students, parents and teachers involved.

SHine is one of the few examples of a program designed in reaction to current research and then followed up by more research to prove its efficacy. When I read through its curriculum it was clear that none of it is new or controversial. Why aren't lessons in sexual diversity standard in every high school? Why aren't all teenagers taught about consent and negotiation? Why are we not teaching young people that sex should always, always, always be pleasurable to both parties? When are we going to wake up to the fact that teaching sixteen-year-olds how to make a baby is less useful than teaching them how to bring themselves to orgasm?

Our sexualised culture is not going to go away, no matter how many of us wish it would. And the urge for teenagers to have sex is not going to disappear. The best defence against a culture that threatens to corrupt young people is through sex education. The surest way of ensuring teenagers emerge into adulthood relatively unscathed by raunch culture, by the commercialisation of sexuality and by plain old difficult, confusing adolescence, is to teach them that our sexuality is integral to who we are, that it is different for everyone, and that no one has the right to impose their version of it on anyone else.

5
Bachelor Gals and Bitter Spinsters

My on-again, off-again relationship with marriage

My decision to wed, at the preposterous age of twenty, was a source of great amusement to my parents and friends who had for years heard me rail against the institution of marriage. My siblings remembered a time even further back (as siblings are always able to do) when I declared I would be married on horseback, in a graveyard, wearing trousers and with my face painted white. On my actual wedding day (cream and gold brushed-satin dress, four bridesmaids, armfuls of lilies, many teary speeches) these anecdotes seemed cute; ten years later both the wedding and the stories told on that day make me feel queasy.

More than that, the idea of marriage itself makes me uncomfortable.

Although I am more in love with my husband now than on the day I married him, if I was making the decision today I would choose not to get married. As nicely as things have turned out, I realise I was right as a teenager: sexist, heterosexist and socially conservative, marriage doesn't have a lot going for it.

Although it's easy to understand why the twenty-year-old me got married (idealism, naivety, hormones, short-lived phase of traditionalism), I'm baffled over why the bookish tomboy me with no interest in boys or clothes or babies was planning her alt-goth nuptial extravaganza at the age of ten. Was I inspired by the twenty-four-hour Diana-Charles fest to create an anti-princess wedding? Did someone ask me how I wanted my wedding to be? Why didn't I respond, as I did six or seven years later, by stating I would not marry at all? What made such a staunchly unromantic, un-girly girl create a wedding fantasy, however unconventional?

Another question: why, twenty years after I fantasised my wedding, fifteen years after I swore I wouldn't have one, and ten years after I said 'I do', *why* am I still so conflicted about what it means to be married?

The pressure to marry

Single women are husband-stealers, home-wreckers or emasculating bitches. Or they are lonely, pathetic, cat-owning, pillow-embroidering spinsters. ('The news that 51 percent of all women live without a spouse might be enough to make you invest in cat futures', is how the *New York Times* introduced a 21 January 2007 story.) They are desperate, grasping husband-hunters ('From Trophy Wife to Toxic Wife!' screamed London's *Telegraph*) or they are vengeful man-haters. ('Watch out Men! More Women Opt to Live Alone,' warned MSNBC.) Almost every newspaper or magazine article discussing unmarried women refers to the long-over pop culture moments of 'Sex and the City', *Bridget Jones* or 'Ally McBeal'.

Although negative stereotypes abound, the life of a single woman today is immeasurably better than it would have been for her mother or grandmother. It has become increasingly acceptable for a woman to live alone or with friends, rather than go straight from the home of her father to that of her husband (de facto or official). Access to contraception and abortion means the unmarried woman can enjoy sex without fear of pregnancy or disease; access to a wider range of education and career opportunities means she need not rely on a husband to put a roof over her head and food on the table. And, just as today's professional woman is not confined to the role of teacher, nun or nurse, today's single woman does not create a scandal if she decides to eat out, take a holiday or buy a house all alone. Being single today is nowhere near the social and financial nightmare it was even thirty-five years ago.

In fact, looking at her situation legally, professionally, politically and socially, the single woman probably has more freedom and opportunities than any other group. No, that's not exactly right. I should say the single woman *under the age of thirty-five* probably has more freedom and greater opportunities than any other group.

Once she turns thirty-five, or earlier in some circles, she may as well be living in 1955. Suddenly, she is desperate and sad, rather than free-spirited and independent. The media, politicians and well-meaning friends and relatives tell her in an urgent tone that married women are happier, healthier and wealthier; that the odds of conceiving drop dramatically after thirty-five and that the chances of marrying drop likewise. ('Unfortunately, as a woman ages, she may become less desirable because of both her decrease in fertility and the scrutiny of a youth-obsessed culture,' clucks an article in *Madison* magazine as recently as February 2007.) She is warned, in short, that if she insists on staying single her chances of future happiness will shrivel along with her womb, heart and social status.

'I like being single,' says Sara, a thirty-six-year-old Brisbane retail manager. 'But by God I'm sick of having to explain my life to every random person I'm so much as introduced to. People I've known less then ten minutes ask me the most intrusive questions: Why am I alone? Don't I like men? Have I been badly hurt in the past?'

Hilary, a thirty-year-old TV researcher from Sydney, tells a similar story. 'It's like a disease. If you're single and there's a random single guy, people assume you must want to be together. Like, "Meet Jeffrey, he's single." Yeah, and he's bald, short and he smokes. And he's forty...A lot of people don't understand how you can be happy and single.'

Hilary's best friend Clare, a thirty-one-year-old high school teacher, has had several long-term relationships and would love to start a family, but she is not willing to compromise in order to do so. She's hurt and frustrated by the reactions of others around her.

> There's so much discrimination of single people. [My colleagues]... tease me incessantly about being single, and could I ever say back to them, 'Oh, how's your loveless marriage going?' I could never do that. But it's completely socially acceptable to say, 'Found a boyfriend yet?'...It's like there's something wrong with me because I haven't been snapped up...The one thing I really envy about

> married people is they don't have to keep putting themselves out there, embarrassing themselves. Listening to people say 'Oh, is this one going to work out?' You're playing out already difficult situations in front of an audience.

Why so much pressure on women to marry? Well, a single woman is frightening to some people because she is an unknown quantity. She might be a student, a CEO, a mother, a lesbian, a party girl. She might be all of these at once. She could go on welfare and suck the system dry, because she has no husband to support her many children or her layabout, druggy lifestyle. She could work twelve hours a day and pay scads of tax and spend her weekends (when wives are attending soccer matches and cooking roast dinners) feeding the homeless or writing political pamphlets. She might be a powerful consumer or a drain on the economy. She might steal your husband or break your son's heart or fill your wife with envy with her satisfying, independent lifestyle. She might be any of these things or none of them. She could do anything!

Added to this fear is the drive amongst social and political conservatives to have women revert to traditional roles. If you believe that a woman's natural role is as a homemaker and mother, then every childless, single woman of reproductive age becomes a threat to the natural order. If you believe in minimalist government, with a corresponding minimalist welfare budget, it is expedient to have married women revert to traditional roles as carers of children and the elderly, with a bit of volunteer work helping the poor.

Research in 2006 by the Academy of Social Sciences of Australia suggests hours spent in informal (but necessary) care, such as home care for the elderly and the disabled, is equivalent to one million full-time jobs in a country with a population of twenty million people. In the past, these unpaid hours have been overwhelmingly performed by women. Now that legal and economic barriers to educational and work opportunities have been mostly broken down, marriage is still the best way society has of encouraging women to conform to these traditional roles.

The myth of the unmarriageable feminist

Consider the ideology behind some recently published words, from ostensibly progressive sources, about the role of the wife. 'Guys: A word of advice,' wrote *Forbes.com* editor Michael Noer in August 2006: 'Marry pretty women or ugly ones. Short ones or tall ones. Blondes or brunettes. Just, whatever you do, don't marry a woman with a career.' According to Noer, if men ignore his advice and marry a 'career girl' they will find themselves living in dirty houses, cuckolded, childless, ill and ultimately divorced. Oh, and by 'career girl' he means anyone with a tertiary education who earns over US$30,000 a year and works more than thirty-five hours a week. (What is it with that 'career girl' phrase? Are the men Noer is advising 'career boys'?)

By these criteria, almost every woman I know is unmarriageable. It's simply bogus to blame problems in two-career relationships on women. If the competing demands of two careers are creating conflict in a relationship, why should women be the ones to abandon ambition in order to keep the peace at home?

Besides, Noer himself makes reference to studies showing 'that working outside the home actually increases marital stability...when the marriage is a happy one'. He goes on to complain that 'even in these studies, wives' employment does correlate positively to divorce rates, when the marriage is of low marital quality'. In other words, happily married women don't file for divorce but unhappily married women might if they have the means to support themselves financially. It seems some men would prefer to have a trapped wife than no wife at all.

Susan Maushart, in her book *Wifework* (2001), presents convincing research that shows most married women end up doing more than an equal share of household tasks, and that men receive far more benefit from marriage than women do. Given this, one can understand why Noer and like-minded men might want to hang on to a wife whether she wants to be there or not.

Maushart, a feminist, argues from the opposite position to Noer but both seem to believe that most men would prefer an unhappy housewife to no housewife at all. This is, in my opinion, a significant overstatement. Yes, many wives find themselves nudged by extended family expectations and cultural pressures into performing traditional domestic roles. But most women who resist the slide into 1950s wifedom will have the support of their husband. Few men these days want a wife who is more Mummy than Partner.

Nobody seems to have told one-time feminist icon Fay Weldon this. Common themes in Weldon's early novels were the misery of economic dependence on a man and the necessity for women to have independent means of support. So it was disappointing to hear that she had written, in her 2006 book *What Makes Women Happy*, that the secret to holding on to a husband is faking orgasms. Women, according to Weldon, are born to be the caretakers of men's egos even at the expense of their own happiness. When a woman 'insists on' an orgasm it makes a man 'anxious and so less able to perform'. The 'kind' thing to do, therefore, is 'fake it and then leap out of bed and pour him champagne, telling him, "You are so clever" or however you express enthusiasm'. Weldon underestimates the level of satisfaction most men get from knowing their partners are sexually satisfied too. She seems to believe that men would prefer a deceitful, self-martyring wife to a genuinely enthusiastic sexual partner.

Weldon also says that 'career women' are likely to end up alone. She obviously hasn't seen the results of a University of Wisconsin study, published in February 2001 in the *Journal of Sex Research*, indicating that sexual satisfaction is highest for men and women in marriages where both partners work and have a high satisfaction level in their work. Or the Australian National University study in 2007 that found married men's happiness increased along with their wives' education levels. There are plenty of studies showing that men prefer women with high earning capacity and that marriages are happier when the wife has a university education.

But so what? Reports that men *do* like smart women play into the same conservative assumptions as those that men *don't* like smart women. Both kinds of report assume that women should care: that we should pretend we can't read more than a cookbook, or apply for a higher paying job and enrol in a post-graduate degree. Most significantly, both kinds assume that it is the responsibility of women to make themselves marriageable. The information is provided as though it were a social service: ladies, listen up, the future of marriage is in your hands.

Jillian Straus's 2007 book, *Unhooked Generation*, is a case in point.

Straus details the 'Seven Evil Influences' that are apparently keeping Generation X women single, one of which is, of course, feminism. Straus prefaces this section by saying she considers 'feminism a spectacular influence' and it is only the 'inadvertent effects of feminism' that are keeping Gen Xers single. What are these 'inadvertent effects'? Well, thanks to feminism 'we have multiple choices, but not multiple lives, and the message is that in one life we can't do it all'. This is true enough as far as it goes, but it is beside the point. First, having multiple choices is not an inadvertent effect of feminism, it's a central, vital aim. Second, so what? Most of us—women and men—have more choices than we can exercise in one lifetime. That no human being can 'do it all' is nothing to do with feminism: it's life.

There is no need to panic about the fact that women, like men, can now choose the direction of their own lives. There is nothing alarming about the fact that young women, like young men, can now make all kinds of stupid, irresponsible decisions they will live to regret, as well as all kinds of wonderful adventurous choices that will shape their entire lives. Women, like men, can consider options and live with the consequences. Women, like men, get smarter and tougher after making a few mistakes and taking a few risks. Women, like men, are better partners, friends, parents—better *people*—if they have survived the panicky sense of free-falling that self-dependence can, at first, create.

Women's magazines and self-help books often advise single women that independence and confidence are qualities they should nurture as they search for a partner. But these qualities are pitched as important because they will help catch a man, rather than important in their own right. ('Any guy will tell you that confidence is sexy, so work on yourself and you'll attract more positive attention,' according to a recent *Cleo* article titled 'Down with the Husband Hunt'.) And since these attributes are useful only for the purposes of fooling a man into liking you, they need not be genuine qualities. According to the women's magazine philosophy of man-hunting, you can obtain Respect and Confidence the same way you get everything else in this consumer society: through purchasing stuff or performing roles.

The right outfit and facial expression may make a woman appear strong, but nothing will make her strong except living through a couple of tough life experiences. Playing hard-to-get may make a woman seem independent, but she will only be independent if she makes decisions based on what she wants to get out of life (and sometimes this may mean playing very-easy-to-get). A diamond ring makes a woman appear loved, but it will never stop her from feeling lonely or unworthy or ugly or sad. And marriage will turn a woman into a wife, but it will never turn a directionless woman into one with a purpose.

What's the point?

Although our culture pushes the idea that marriage is obligatory for adults, being single is not odd or selfish or empowering or anything in particular; it's being single. It takes no special effort and is the default unless you decide otherwise. Marriage, on the other hand, won't happen without momentous decisions being made by two people, and it won't last long without their continued enormous effort.

And of course marriage isn't necessary even if you have met someone with whom you want to live and love forever. It's perfectly possible to have a happy, committed, loving relationship without any kind of ceremony or signature. Marriage should be an option, sure, because some of us love a party or crave ceremony or desire public recognition of our relationship. But to treat it as the destiny of all responsible adults, or as something to which all women should aspire, is ridiculous.

From a pragmatic viewpoint, however, there are plenty of reasons to get married. According to the US Government Accounting Office married people potentially benefit over single people in 1100 ways, including a better deal on taxes, healthcare and property ownership. These benefits may vary in detail and quantity, but in most countries marriage provides legal and economic benefits. Then there are the less tangible benefits: public recognition of and respect for your relationship and the avoidance of social stigma for your children.

These benefits are partly legal and partly cultural and there are plenty of arguments in favour of dismantling the inequality between those who currently can and can't marry. But what if a person's economic, legal and social status was to remain unchanged whether they get married or not. Would anyone still get married? The prevalence of same-sex marriages suggests that the answer is yes. Same-sex marriages are not legally recognised (in Australia and most of the US) and so do not confer the same benefits as heterosexual marriage.

I recently attended the wedding of two people who—being in their early thirties and committed to family and community—should have been the poster-models for any government campaign designed to raise the marriage rate. The ceremony was held in a Melbourne park on a freezing, stormy July day. The sun came out for only forty-five minutes that day, and that forty-five minutes happened to coincide exactly with the bridal procession and exchange of vows. Some people said this was proof God smiled on the wedding. I don't go in for that, but it was a lovely coincidence.

The hundred or so guests stood in that brief, beautiful sunshine and watched as the brides, both wearing blinding white gowns and sparkling tiaras, promised to love, honour and care for each other for the rest of their lives. I'd known one of the brides for eighteen years and had never seen her look so alive. I was meeting her wife for the first time, but everything about her made me realise she was the absolute perfect partner for my dear friend.

At the reception, two old men danced cheek to cheek, the mother of one of the brides spun her newborn granddaughter around the room, various small children ducked in between feet, aunties and uncles propped up the bar with school friends, and lesbian activists did the Macarena with Catholic school teachers. Students of one of the brides made the rest of us feel old and slow on the dance floor. The decorations and cake were red and white—the colours of both brides' birth nations' flags—and so we celebrated the coming together of cultures as well as families. We celebrated friendship and kinship and history and the future and love. We celebrated a marriage, no more, no less.

For several years I've been asking myself whether marriage can be feminist and this wedding helped me come to an answer. Of course it can—it can be anything married people make it. But the way mainstream culture defines marriage is decidedly *un*feminist and so it can be far more difficult than many brides anticipate not to slide into the traditional role of 'wife'. It can also be far more difficult than it should be to resist marriage—feminist or otherwise.

Given our cultural love of marriage, it is unrealistic to expect it to disappear anytime soon. The way forward, then, is to work at expanding the meaning of marriage so that gender and sexual orientation are less important than love and commitment. Marriage has always changed in reaction to society changing, and will continue to change as people change—married people and those who want to be married.

Which is why, despite its questionable past, and its discriminatory and sometimes ludicrous present, marriage thrives. Marriage is invented anew by each couple who makes vows; it's reinvented when a child is born, a job is lost, illness or tragedy strikes. I got married out of naivety and a misdirected craving for adventure and romance. I stay married for completely different reasons and these reasons change as I change, as my husband changes. We're constantly re-engaging, constantly re-assessing, re-committing. We got married once, but we choose to stay married every day.

In the words of the poet Marge Piercy, 'We cannot invent a language of new grunts. We start where we find ourselves, at this time and place'. Marriage is what we have; what we do with it is up to us.

6
Desperate Housewives and Natural Mothers

No one needs to be a housewife

Housework, Betty Friedan wrote over forty years ago, 'can hardly use the abilities of a woman of average or normal human intelligence'. Although it's possible to make it more interesting by baking soufflés rather than slapping down rissoles, or more challenging by hand-sewing every item of clothing, or more time-consuming by ironing the undies, most of what we call housework could be performed, as Friedan wrote, 'by an eight-year-old child'.

I'm not advocating child labour as a solution to the domestic time crunch; I'm saying that keeping a house liveable and a kitchen stocked does not have to be difficult or overly time-consuming. A little bit of clutter or grime isn't going to kill anyone. Relax your standards and make everyone in the house pitch in.

Or don't. The ultra-perfect June-Cleaver-Martha-Stewart thing might give you pleasure, in which case, go right ahead, but understand it is a luxury—a nice hobby, if you will. Cleaning and maintaining one regular family home is not a full-time job. Professional cleaners manage to do several every day.

Parenting is a different matter. There's no denying that good parenting requires love, skill, maturity and care, and that most kids benefit from having at least one parent intimately involved in their lives. What form this involvement takes varies from family to family and from life-stage to life-stage, and so it should. Babies require a different level and kind of care from toddlers who have different needs from primary schoolers who are a different species altogether from teenagers. And within age-groups, the needs of children—and the capabilities of parents to fulfil those needs—vary dramatically.

So when one mother tells me her children would be better off if she worked full-time because she would be happier and more fulfilled, I believe her. When another tells me she would be heartbroken if she had to leave her baby daughter each day to go back to work, I believe her, too. When my mother, whose career has been both personally fulfilling and valuable to the community, tells me that raising her four children is the most important thing she's ever done, I believe her. There is no contradiction between her commitment to her children and her working full-time for most of our childhood.

The childcare/career issue is not, as it is so often presented, an either/or issue. Childcare is incredibly important *and* it may not be the best use of the bulk of every parent's time. It is difficult *and*, for many people, immensely fulfilling. It is something most women care about *and* it is not—absolutely definitively *not*—only a 'women's issue'.

Full-time mothering is awesome (even if mothers say it isn't)

On an unusually hot September morning I visited a playgroup held in a well maintained shady playground in Sydney's Sutherland Shire. Ten of the twelve mothers first met at a mothers' clinic when their children were newborn and they went on to form this playgroup together. The eldest of these babies was now eighteen months old. Four of the original ten women were pregnant for a second time, one recently miscarried and one had a six-week-old baby. All were between twenty-four and thirty-five years of age and married.

Every woman at the playgroup was the partner with the primary responsibility for childcare and domestic work in her household, which was to be expected, as none of the women worked full-time, while all of their husbands did. I asked the women how they liked full-time parenting. Without any further prompting, they spoke for almost an hour, interrupting and talking over the top of each other in their enthusiasm to be heard.

Their answers echoed those given in the 2004 Monash University study *What Women (and Men) Want: Births, Policies and Choices*. Most of the women in that study felt that 'mothers were not accorded a high status position and that their social contribution was not always valued'. The women at playgroup told me they felt 'unappreciated', 'degraded' and 'invisible'. 'Exhausted', 'bored', 'lonely' and 'depressed' also came up a lot. 'Nobody values the work we do,' said one woman. 'I mean, I don't even value it. When people ask me what I do, I don't know what to say.'

I told the women that I had often observed the opposite; that mothers, particularly full-time stay-at-home mothers, seemed to be idolised in our culture. I'm always hearing that a mother's job is the most important and fulfilling in the world. For a childless woman it can be galling and even hurtful. My decision not to have children was made after deep consideration over an extended period, yet I'm constantly told (often by people who barely know me) that I am making a terrible mistake. The message is that if I don't go against my own instincts, and my own reasoning, and become a mother, I will never reach my full potential. Motherhood, I'm told, is the ultimate achievement for a woman. For every woman.

'It's just stuff people say to cover up how much it sucks,' said a woman who appears the epitome of fulfilled motherhood. She is thirty-two years old, tertiary educated and beautiful in a sun-kissed, just popping out for a game of tennis and a wheatgrass juice way. Her child is polite and affectionate, playing sweetly with the others, stopping only to eat the fresh fruit salad her mother has prepared.

'You hear some women say "Oh, I'm a domestic goddess" or "I'm the CEO of my household",' she went on. 'I know why they do it, but it's embarrassing. Call yourself a "managing director of household activities" and I guarantee other people will hear "insecure housewife".'

'It's frustrating,' said another woman, who had just wiped her toddler's nose for the sixth or seventh time that morning. 'If it's all so empowering and satisfying why aren't more men doing it? What, they're all so unselfish and self-sacrificing that they leave the most special, rewarding work to the women?'

I thought of her words a little over a month later, while reading an opinion piece by journalist Jim Schembri in the *Age*. He relates that he 'went ballistic' when a female friend who has recently become a full-time mum told him she was 'suffering from relevance deprivation being stuck to the sink at home with the kids'. In response, Schembri 'half-screamed' that far from being irrelevant or a chore, motherhood 'is the single most important thing a person can do'. Predictably enough, he goes on to blame feminism for giving motherhood a bad name. I wonder if his friend was as gobsmacked as I was at the way this man ignored her experience as a stay-at-home mother, in favour of lecturing her on how she *should* feel about it. I wonder if his friend felt, as I did, that Schembri should go ahead and be a full-time parent himself if he thought it was so wonderful.

To tell a woman how she *should* feel and then to blame feminism when the woman says she *doesn't* feel that way is bad enough, but then Schembri and other conservative commentators compound their arrogance by pretending their intention is to compliment the woman. It's a way of defending the domestic gender imbalance with a disingenuous argument of female supremacy. You know the line: men are so useless you can't possibly expect them to know how to use the washing machine/do the grocery shopping/bath the toddler and so on.

Even though this kind of rhetoric sounds like it's all about female superiority—*women are clever and competent, men are fumbling fools*—it's as sexist at heart as the rhetoric that claims *all men are beasts so women must cover up to prevent themselves being raped*. The cult of female domestic superiority talks up women but only in the context of traditional roles. *Women are born to this stuff*, it says. *When you mess with nature, you get overflowing washing machines and kids with bellyaches.*

But you're so much better at it...

Even progressive couples, who see through the 'men are useless with kids' nonsense and commit themselves to non-sexist parenting, sometimes show evidence of an ingrained belief that childcare is women's business. New mothers compare experiences with other mothers, read books and websites and ask advice from doctors and baby-care nurses. They often feel incompetent and out of their depth but they persist in asking for help, trying new things, learning and practising, and over time they become the expert on what their child needs. Very few mothers will tell you that it all came naturally. And very few fathers will tell you they worked as hard on learning how to care for a newborn, and how to assess and respond to the child's growth and development. Little surprise then, that when it comes to childcare, many men find that 'she's just better at that stuff'.

A friend told me she realised she was kidding herself about her husband being equally involved in childcare when she found herself writing a list of instructions before leaving him alone with their eighteen-month-old. 'Instructions are for babysitters,' she said. 'A parent should know what his kid eats and at what time. He should know as well as I do what time she goes down for a nap.'

A similarly gendered blind spot is evident in many couples' decision about which partner (if either) will stay at home with the kids.

Many of the mothers I talked to told me they didn't work because their after-tax salary would barely cover the cost of full-time childcare. 'It's not worth it,' they all said. I don't know exactly how much these women or their husbands earned, but it was obvious they weren't deducting half, or indeed any, of the childcare cost from their husband's salary. The calculation seemed to be: Woman's Salary – Childcare = Might as Well Stay Home. Shouldn't it go: Family Income – Childcare = New Family Income if we Both Decide to Work?

A report on the 'financial reality for working mothers', which appeared in the *Age* in January 2006, suffers from the same limits. While the article, titled 'Why Do They Do It?', thoroughly examines the various reasons women give for returning to full- or part-time work versus staying home with their children, their partners are mentioned only in passing. The article includes analyses of four women's financial situations, including her income, less tax, travel costs and childcare costs. Income earned by the fathers is conspicuously absent from the equations.

Few couples think to debate whether it is 'worth it' or 'best for the baby' if the father gives up his job. Some men do take on a full-time parenting role, but they are still exceptional enough to cause comment. Often, too, these men will say that they were never particularly invested in their job and so it was no hardship to give up paid work. The implication is that these men would not have considered abandoning successful, lucrative, fulfilling jobs to care for their child. Most working mothers do not have the luxury of only leaving work if they don't want to be there anyway. However much you love your job, however successful you are professionally, there is always the pressure—sometimes subtle and unspoken, sometimes loud and aggressive—to dump the career in order to devote your full attention to parenting.

Sisterhood vs. motherhood?

In January 2007, the former Australian Prime Minister John Howard told a newspaper columnist that:

> Fortunately, I think today's younger women are more in the post-feminist period, where they don't measure their independence and freedom by the number of years they remain full-time in the work-force without having children...I think they have moved on from that sort of demonstration phase, in the sense of 'I'll be letting the sisterhood down if I don't stay in the workforce until I'm a certain age.' I think they are more confident.

Howard's comment gives the impression that no mother would choose to work full-time if not for the incredible pressure inflicted by 'the sisterhood'. His assumption is that women's natural role is motherhood and the professional gains made by women in the last thirty years were a failed social experiment that is, mercifully, coming to an end.

Anne Manne, in her 2005 book, *Motherhood*, argues that mothers should commit to staying at home because children need maternal care. She argues that the 'rights of mothers' to pursue their careers impede upon the rights of children. Although her book contains a good amount of discussion about the need for more family-friendly workplaces and better government support for families, it is weakened by the underlying assumption that a mother, rather than a loving parent/guardian of either gender, is what children need.

Manne tells anecdote after anecdote about children who appear sad when separated from their mothers, but none about children who look upset when their father leaves for the day. I could come up with a few examples of kids who miss their dads, but so what? As Leslie Cannold asks in a review of *Motherhood*, 'Is the pain of missing a beloved other than a mother good enough reason to change care arrangements too?'

The whole debate rests on the flawed premise that only women have children. But most people in the workforce are, or will be, parents. It's ridiculous, then, that most workplaces are structured as though *nobody* is a parent. Whenever an argument is made for better parental leave provisions or increased work-hour flexibility, employer groups react with horror, as though women are ruining everything for everyone. But—this needs to be repeated until everyone gets it—men are parents too. If they're not as concerned about juggling childcare and work as women, then they should be!

And those who, like me, are not parents and never intend to be must recognise that the children of our colleagues will one day be our employees, our politicians, economists, plumbers, teachers and doctors—our future. American author Ann Crittenden points out in her book, *The Price of Motherhood*, that 'two-thirds of all wealth is created by human skills, creativity, and enterprise'. Children, Crittenden says, quoting economist Shirley Burggraf, are 'the major wealth producers in our economy'.

One for the country

Attitudes about women as the natural carers of children are compounded, encouraged, and perhaps reflected in, government and workplace policy. Author and academic Anne Summers, in her 2003 book *The End of Equality*, wrote that Australian federal social policy is based on 'the breeding creed', an ideology that 'defines women first and foremost as mothers and aims to subsume all of women's other choices and ambitions into a motherhood mentality'. She was talking about recent initiatives such as the $4000 lump-sum paid on the birth of each baby, a taxation system favouring single-income families, the lack of funding and tax-deductible status for childcare, Australia's position as one of only two developed nations (the other is the US) to have no statutory paid maternity leave, and the astonishing calls in 2004 from the former Treasurer, Peter Costello, for women to 'have one for mum, one for dad, and one for the country'.

The Treasurer's outburst revealed the ultimate aim of much of that government's family policy: to reverse the declining birthrate. It seems to have worked: 2006 Australian Bureau of Statistics figures showed the highest birthrate since 1971. Australian National University demographer Peter McDonald said of the increase that, although 'the maternity payment has had a financial impact…the social message that it sends, that is, that if you have children, the Government values your contribution to society' was probably more significant.

It doesn't seem to be in any country's direct interests to promote policies which concentrate on birth numbers rather than the well-being of families and the autonomy of women. The 2006 *Parental Leave in Australia Survey* of parents with children under the age of two found that a fifth of the women who left the workforce to be a full-time parent after their child's birth cited lack of paid maternity leave as their reason for quitting. Around 50 percent of respondents said that better parental leave provisions 'would have improved things most for them in the period since the birth of their child', and a similar percentage said better childcare provisions 'would have improved things most for them in the period since the birth of their child'. Thirty-nine percent of all families specifically identified 'more affordable childcare' as something that would have improved their situation.

There's plenty of evidence that improved parenting leave and childcare provisions would not only make combining work and family easier, but would increase the national birthrate without having to resort to lump-sum bribes. As American writer and researcher Sharon Lerner puts it, 'the promotion of larger families and the promotion of women's careers may go hand in hand'. Lerner posits that this 'fertility paradox' is caused by the fact that societies based on the old family model struggle to cope when women go to work. 'With little public support for working mothers forthcoming, women are likely to think they must choose work or motherhood.'

Two outstanding European examples are Norway and France, both of which have high (by European standard) birthrates *and* high rates of female participation in the workforce. Norwegian mothers can choose between twelve months off work at 80 percent pay, or ten months with full pay. A new father can opt to take most of the leave instead of the mother, and he *must* take at least four weeks or that paid time is lost to the couple. France spends 15 percent of its national budget on family leave and childcare provisions, because, according to the French Ministry of Family Affairs, it is committed to giving 'priority to reconciling family life and professional life. We want to encourage births and permit women to work if they want.'

Lerner points out that Europe's lowest birthrates belong to Spain, Portugal, Italy and Greece, nations in which old social ideas about women as mothers first, workers second, if at all, are reflected in public policy. While these countries do better than the US and Australia in guaranteeing at least some maternity leave, none comes close to the Norwegian or French provisions and none has guaranteed paternity leave.

No woman is an island

In 2004, Kristie Brown of the Australian Women's Electoral Lobby reported the results of interviews she conducted with women aged eighteen to twenty-four as part of her honours thesis. She found that young women considered themselves 'people not genders', that they didn't think being female affected their opportunities or choices and that they 'vigorously rejected' the label 'feminist' and the idea that women are oppressed. Yet the same young women felt they 'did not have equality in the domestic sphere' and that 'gender could become an issue when it came to housework and raising children'.

Our culture is individualistic; it values personal agency and responsibility. Accordingly, we all like to think we make rational choices based on nothing but our personal needs and desires, and we like to think we can cop the consequences of those decisions. Nobody wants to be seen as a whinger, blaming her problems on society or the government or 'the system'. Thus, most women claim it is their choice to stay at home with the kids, and the larger forces that may be influencing or even forcing their particular 'choice' are ignored.

The decision whether to work outside of the home *is* a private one, but the construction of a society that makes it difficult for most parents to manage work and family responsibilities is a matter of concern. The authors of the *What Women (and Men) Want* study concluded that:

> particular policy initiatives and entitlements did not influence singularly the decisions made about fertility, but they did form the landscape in which women and men negotiated their choices about families, work and life. Rather than operating as a direct inducement, policy initiatives formed the backdrop that encouraged and shaped women's decisions…

The authors wrote that 'many women ended up lowering their expectations about what both governments and employers would provide in supporting their fertility decisions'. As anyone who has ever tried to get out of something by doing a crappy job knows, fostering low expectations is a fantastic way to ensure that not much will be asked of you in the future. If women have low expectations of their workplaces and governments, these same women will struggle through on their own, not bothering to agitate or even ask for a better deal from the workplace or society.

The resistance to structural change in corporate and social policy is disheartening, but the worst thing women can do is sigh and get on with things; we need to change these outdated attitudes. We need to shout about the fact that gender roles are constructs. We need to spread the word that women are not naturally better parents than men (with the exception of breastfeeding). Parenting tasks, outside of grunt work, require a set of *learned* skills. Women often have learnt these skills from their mothers or have absorbed them from a culture which tells them they need to know this stuff. We know that men are capable of learning how to raise children because lots of them already do it and do it well. But many more still don't bother to learn because their female partners absolve them of the need by taking it all on themselves.

Why women's careers matter

It doesn't matter if we manage to eliminate gender discrimination in the workplace—if mothers are still assumed to be the natural caregivers of children then women will never fill the half of senior paid positions they should, by rights, fill. Even the most progressive, family-friendly workplace will suffer gender disparity at the upper levels of management if more women than men take years off to raise children: years in which their male colleagues are gaining the kind of experience that will see them promoted to the top jobs.

Ann Crittenden writes in *The Price of Motherhood* that 'motherhood is the single greatest risk factor for poverty among American women', and several American studies have shown that professional women who return to full-time work after time off or a period of part-time work suffer a substantial cut in pay and responsibility. In Australia, John von Doussa, the president of the Human Rights and Equal Opportunity Commission, pointing to the low level of women's workforce participation and earnings (about 84 percent of men's), said that 'women are getting punished for the simple fact that they, genetically, are those with the function to produce the next generation'.

The dean of Yale College, Peter Salovey, in a recent *New York Times Magazine* article about the ambitions of female college students, was quoted as being worried that 'so few students seem to be able to imagine a life for themselves that isn't constructed along traditional gender roles'. This is indeed a serious problem. Every little girl who dreams of being a wife and mother has plenty of role models to choose from, but not so for the girl who wants to be a scientist or CEO or judge.

Role models matter even more to young women starting in their careers. In 1990, a Law Institute of Victoria study found that although women make up 50 percent of law graduates, articled law clerks and first-year solicitors, they comprise only 23 percent of lawyers in private firms and 12 percent of partners in private law firms. Fifteen years later, the Victorian Women Lawyers Association reported that although women and men continue to be represented equally in the legal profession as a whole, women still account for only 14 percent of partners in private practice. In other words, there are few examples for young women wanting to move into the more lucrative and prestigious areas of the law. In the business world, according to the 2007 International Business Report, only a quarter of senior management positions are held by women, while more than one-third of Australian businesses have no women at all in senior roles.

The *National Study of the Changing Workforce*, conducted every five years by the US Families and Work Institute, found in its 2002 survey that two in five men, and almost as many women, agreed with the statement 'men should earn the money and women should stay at home minding the house and children'. Eighty-three percent of New

Zealanders, surveyed by the International Social Survey Programme in 2006 about work and family, said they approved of childless married women working full-time compared to a shockingly low 2 percent who approved of women with under-school-age children working full-time and an only slightly better 14 percent who approved of women with school-age children working full-time. Does anyone really think that these attitudes are not formed and fostered in the home, that the men and women surveyed here did not grow up with the idea that Mummy takes care of the kids and Daddy earns the money?

Girls raised with the expectation that they will one day quit work to raise children are less likely to take their educations or their early jobs seriously. Why bother working to top your university course or gain early promotion if you're only going to drop out of the professional world in a few years anyway? Boys raised with the understanding that they will be able to enjoy fatherhood without interrupting their careers for a microsecond will see female colleagues of reproductive age as time-bombs, and will expect them to retire to their inherited role once they become pregnant. Why train and promote women if they will only leave when the time comes to start a family?

So young women are not mentored and challenged and advanced in the same way men are, which means that when the time comes to make a childcare decision it may well be true that the female partner's career prospects and earnings are less spectacular than the male's and so it 'makes sense' for her to stay at home. Thus the perception that women drop out when they have children is reinforced. And there are few women staying in the workforce agitating for change, so no change happens, and the next generation of women faces the same shitty choices and everybody's assumptions are reinforced again.

Any advances made in the area of gender roles and parenting have been the result of women refusing to give in to the presumption that childcare is exclusively their problem, and also of men refusing to go along with the idea that their sole contribution to their kids' upbringing is financial. Every time a woman decides it's too hard, she makes it harder for the next woman to face the same choices. The workplace will not change unless more women make the choice to stay and fight.

7
The Body Trap

Learning to be an object

I remember very clearly the moment I understood that puberty was a public event, that my life would be affected by my body's changes whether or not I decided to use my new facilities to incubate, deliver and feed babies. I was thirteen and although I already wore a bra and had been menstruating for over a year, I didn't give much thought to my body as an object.

I was waiting for the school bus, looking blindly at the road, my head filled with images from the book I had been reading over breakfast. An older girl sat beside me and said, very kindly, 'You know, most girls your age shave their legs.' I looked down at her slim, tanned, smooth legs and felt deep shame. I had never noticed how disgusting my own legs were: bloated and pasty and covered in hair. I shrugged to show I didn't care, and at home that night I shaved (and repeatedly cut) the legs I now thought of as repulsive.

Over the following months I learnt how to see myself as others did. Within weeks I had exchanged my habit of leisurely reading over a large bowl of Rice Bubbles with honey and banana for a new habit: half a piece of dry toast followed by an hour in front of the mirror, poking, plucking, fixing, despairing. By my fourteenth birthday I had started smoking and working out and had all but stopped eating. In less than a year I went from being oblivious of, to obsessed about my appearance. None of my friends commented on the change in me; they were all going through the same thing.

Puberty, in the words of writer Andi Zeisler, 'is a time when girls by anatomy become girls by imperative'. Suddenly the world has an opinion on how you should be dressed, groomed and shaped. Forget getting used to periods and bras, and start getting used to constant observation and judgment of your every lump, bump, blemish and hair. When you were a kid your body was just what you used to get around and get stuff done; now you're a 'young lady' and your body requires attention from you and should expect attention from others. The hardest thing about this is that although you've inherited the look of a woman (and therefore the inevitable public scrutiny) you've not yet acquired either the legal rights or the earned confidence of an adult.

Boys suffer the pains and humiliations of puberty too, of course. But they don't, for the most part, become public property in the way sexually maturing girls do. Men's bodies are not objects of public consumption to the extent that women's are. Boys need to learn to take care of their new bodies: the inconvenient erections, facial hair that must be shaved even with a face full of painful hormonal pimples, outsized limbs that don't always obey commands. But when they've grown, their new bodies give them a certain power and authority. A man can walk through public spaces with the invisibility of one who belongs. For girls the situation is reversed. A woman's body is a thing to be noticed, commented on, heckled, groped or threatened. Sexual maturity makes a girl's body fair game.

And this never ends. Even the bodies of pregnant women are considered public property; that big belly just screaming out to be touched and commented on by random strangers, your swelling self an invitation to all and sundry to pepper you with advice and urban myths. And when that child is born you better get back to your pre-pregnancy sexiness post-haste if you don't want those affectionate belly rubs and smiles to turn into disgusted grimaces and advice about investing in a jogging stroller. 'Are you a Yummy Mummy or a Slummy Mummy?' asked the UK *Daily Mail* recently, before pointing out you can't possibly be the former if you have a 'saggy tummy'.

Advice, always advice. Every girl and woman of reproductive age is bombarded with advice from the minute she wakes up to the minute she closes her eyes at night. The morning news broadcast includes a segment on the safety of botox; the side of the bus has an ad about slimming down over the summer; your office manager recommends her hairdresser; your assistant says you have to try this new diet; the newspaper has a lift-out on summer fashions, the evening news repeats the morning's botox story and adds one about a new study showing men prefer women with small waists. And that's for those who ignore all the women's magazines and lifestyle programs which exist for the specific purpose of telling women how to make themselves nice.

The message—to state the horribly obvious—is that a woman is never okay as she is. There is always something about you that could be made better, thinner, prettier, smoother, neater, sexier.

In 1991, Naomi Wolf wrote in *The Beauty Myth* that 'The more legal and material hindrances women have broken through, the more strictly and heavily and cruelly images of female beauty have come to weigh upon us.' Wolf argued that the obligation to be beautiful, on top of work and family responsibilities, keeps women too busy, weak and distracted to fight for economic and political equality.

When I first read *The Beauty Myth*, as a teenager, I was stunned. It had never occurred to me that anything other than vanity was behind the beauty-obsessed behaviour of every girl and woman I knew. It was the first time I really understood how the personal was political, although I never would have used the phrase at the time.

I wish I could say that this moment of understanding and the anger that followed changed the way I thought about beauty. I wish I could tell you that, once I realised how cosmetic companies and certain elements of the media were manipulating me into thinking I was ugly so I would buy things, I stopped buying things. I wish I could tell you that, once I realised the time I spent on perfecting my appearance could be better spent working towards equality, I stopped spending time perfecting my appearance. I wish I could report that reading *The Beauty Myth* (and every other feminist book or essay on body image I could find thereafter) changed the way I viewed my own body, but I can't.

This chapter is harder to write than anything else in this book. Since that day at the bus stop I have hated every part of my body, every feature of my face, every centimetre of skin. I have never smiled into a mirror except to check what others might see, to notice the way my eyes wrinkled and my top lip thinned out. I have never seen a photo of myself without feeling despair, followed by fury at myself for being so shallow. I have been on a diet for sixteen years. Occasionally I have gone off it and my screwed-up body has packed on weight within weeks. When I quit smoking I went up two dress sizes in a month. I have since restarted smoking several times because it helps me not eat.

I am a feminist and a harsh critic of our society's insistence on women fitting a particular physical mould. I believe beauty comes in many forms and that a person's appearance has no relationship to their character. I am furious that so many women waste so much time and energy on something so trivial. I am ashamed to admit I am one of them.

A woman can never be too thin or too curvy

Models, popstars and actresses are too thin. The standard they create is unrealistic for ordinary women. So ordinary women and girls end up with low self-esteem and perhaps an eating disorder. It's such a cliché by now that I can hardly bear to contribute to its dissemination one more time. Like most clichés, it also contains a sliver of truth. Most Hollywood types are thinner than is healthy and this does indeed lead to unrealistic expectations amongst those who spend a lot of time observing said entertaining ladies.

There's another cliché that gets wheeled out whenever the first one appears, and it too contains a dollop of truth. This one goes that it's crazy how all those women are starving themselves when everybody knows that men prefer real women with curves. The true bit is that it's crazy those women are starving themselves. That men like curves is also kind-of-sometimes-maybe true, but I'll get to that later.

So there are shreds of truth in these tired old saws, but not nearly enough to excuse their constant, unthinking reproduction in the media: the false concern about the health of shrinking starlets; the pregnancy rumours or ridicule when one of them puts on a pound; the panic over young girls starving themselves to emulate their idols, followed by the ads for diets and plastic surgery; the articles telling girls to respect their bodies and love them just as they are (as long as it's not one of those ugly skinny bodies), followed by the fashion spread using a model who weighs less than a ten-year-old child.

Is it unhealthy to aspire to an unnatural thinness? Of course it is. But how exactly does it help to tell thin girls (or fat girls, for that matter) that men only love curves? Isn't this replacing one ideal image with another? And isn't telling women to be curvaceous because men love it as pathetic as telling girls to be skinny because fashion designers make their clothes really small? Does anyone seriously think that when Marilyn Monroe was the ideal the average woman didn't feel pathetically thin-lipped and flat-chested? If the ideal was a stumpy-legged, pear-shaped, pale-skinned brunette, I'd be a goddess on earth, but most women reading this would still be excluded from the new beauty ideal.

The problem is not with idolising thinness but with presenting any particular body type or skin colour or hair-texture or whatever as a must-attain ideal. We are not supposed to look alike. Imagine proposing that all toddlers should look so similar that you couldn't pick your own kid out of the sandpit. Imagine if the Sunday paper published a feature about how everybody knows that parents love brown-haired babies more than blond ones.

If we can see how wrong-headed and dehumanising the notion of idealised children is, then why can we not see how twisted it is when applied to someone who's twenty or sixteen or forty-three?

The idealisation of a particular shape and size becomes even more ridiculous when we start attributing moral values to physical traits. 'That's a girl who knows how to control herself,' an ex-colleague of mine used to say of an ultra-thin woman in our office, implying that the rest of we fat pigs did not. The connection between self-control and denial would seem obvious: refusing to eat chocolate cake, or even a medium-sized portion of dinner, equals thin. Yet we all know people who are naturally very thin and whose self-control or lack of same has nothing to do with their appearance.

But thin women are not spared the insulting comments and assumptions either. In a recent *Cleo* feature, Australian television comedian and 'Bachelor of the Year' Andy Lee writes:

> Yes, guys might stare at a passing skinny woman, but under no circumstances do we want to be bedding one. To snuggle this non-eating breed of female is like cuddling a skeleton thinly wrapped in Gladwrap...there is no warmth and very little attraction, particularly when Ms Boney takes her clothes off.

Somewhere along the way we got the idea that it is okay to say the most awful things about a thin woman. 'Like cuddling a skeleton.' 'She must be anorexic.' 'I bet she uses drugs to stay that thin.' And, my personal favourite: 'Real women have curves.' Whenever I hear someone say 'real woman' I think of those pseudo-patriots who say they are 'real Australians' or the macho homophobes who think you have to be a beer-swilling womaniser to be a 'real man'. Defining a subset of the population as 'real' implies that anyone who doesn't fit that description is fake, inauthentic, a cheater.

Just as a female person does not need a costume to appear female, a woman's body—whatever its shape or size—is by definition womanly. Those turn-sideways-and-they'll-disappear catwalk models may be starving, or they may have super-speedy metabolisms, but they're all women and they're all real.

Thin is sexy?

Lucia looks more like a catwalk model than an accountant. She is twenty-nine, pale, sad-eyed, with coat-hanger collarbones. Until about eighteen months ago she was, in her own words, 'a porker'. I didn't know her then, but some friends who did know her tell me she was never more than a size 16. So she was overweight but certainly not obese.

'I was normal fat,' she tells me. 'Not like *Biggest Loser* fat.'

Lucia asked our mutual friend to arrange a meeting after she heard I was writing about promiscuous women. As we are settling ourselves on her bed (her flatmates are singing along to *The Sound of Music* in the living room) she tells me she's 'not that much of a slut anymore'.

'It's not as fun now I'm skinny,' she says. 'Men are less inhibited with fat girls. They know you can take it. They're so careful with me now. Like I'll break...I think men like the idea they have to be gentle with a thin girl.'

(I'm reminded of Andy Lee's *Cleo* piece. 'The skinny chick,' he wrote, 'puts considerable pressure on the male during lovemaking. With a fragile frame to work with, the male is forced to tiptoe gently around her in the bedroom, for fear that an overexcited moment of exertion could snap her clean in half.')

'Plus,' Lucia goes on, 'when you're fat people think you must be some hedonist who sits around gorging on cream cakes and whole chickens. Some men assume that you'll be equally decadent in bed so they do stuff they wouldn't think of trying with some delicate little bird they think only eats salad.'

Have all the men she's slept with since losing weight been like this? She nods, then scrunches up her face. 'Not that there's been many. It's such a myth that skinny girls get the guys...You're out at a club or party or whatever, it's getting late...men who want to get laid go straight to the chubby girls. They know they'll be grateful and won't say no. Men don't expect sex from thin girls, not right away anyway... Men who wouldn't have spoken to me in public before but would have fucked me in the toilet cubicle...now they just want to talk and talk and talk. Let all their mates see them with the hot chick. I just know these guys are going home and pounding some fat girl.

'It's weird,' she says. 'I like my body now. I'm stronger and healthier than when I was big. Sex should be better... maybe it will be if I can find a partner who isn't scared of breaking me or corrupting me or whatever it is these guys worry about.'

I don't know if Lucia is extraordinarily cynical and bitter about the singles scene, or if her experience is typical. I do know that our culture objectifies larger women in a bizarre way. Thin may be the beauty standard but it's not necessarily the sexy standard.

When the *Observer Woman Magazine* in the UK ran a photo set of two size 16 models in swimwear, the accompanying editorial had a scandalised tone. When 'we' first saw them, *Observer Woman* writes:

> the photographs seemed illicit, transgressive. They seemed overtly sexual. Fetishistic, almost. They certainly seemed contrary to today's rules on glossy-magazine aesthetics. So much bosom! So much bottom! Such luscious rolls of back fat! Such extravagant thighs! Aren't there laws against this?

Over the top, certainly, but the link between sexuality and fat is commonplace. How many women's mag articles have you read that tell you to be confident about your hips because everyone knows men love women with 'meat on their bones'? I even read one piece of advice that said women who felt self-conscious about their large thighs should look at some porn and realise that men love fleshy bodies. (What they mean, of course, is big breasts.)

The Australian bad-boy journalist Jack Marx wrote a piece for *New Woman* magazine (re-published on his blog) extolling the delights of curvy women. It's a well-intentioned but ultimately clueless rant about how women should accept their flawed bodies because men think their imperfections are sexy. He speaks longingly of a former lover with 'an abundant butt', and muses that this poor girl 'probably looks in the mirror and wishes her butt away, little knowing I'd have happily taken it with me.' It doesn't seem to occur to Marx that what he thinks of her butt (or the bodies of the women he criticises for wearing unflattering clothes in an attempt to look like their fashion idols) doesn't matter a damn. He—like millions of others who write, publish and say this stuff—doesn't grasp that self-acceptance based on a man liking you is no self-acceptance at all.

Disgusting lady bits

One of the biggest gossip stories of 2006 involved pop singer Britney Spears's vulva. Spears, who had recently given birth to her second child and split from the child's father, was out on the town with her friend, amateur porn star and hotel heiress Paris Hilton, when paparazzi managed to snap photos of her without underwear in the back seat of a car. It was an alarming sight: a pre-pubescently smooth vulva inches away from a recent caesarean scar.

One of the fascinating, disturbing and frustrating aspects of the public reaction to the incident was the way Spears's vulva was referred to. Girly bits, lady bits, crotch and vagina were the most common printable terms. Nobody, it seemed, wanted to use the correct term for the flashed part: vulva.

The vagina, for those who should know but don't, is the inside part, the part you can only see with a torch and a speculum. The vulva is the outside part, the part you wax and then flash at friendly paparazzi when you're out on the town. Whenever I hear someone refer to what Britney flashed as a shaved or waxed vagina I squeeze my legs together and wince. Can you imagine pouring hot wax into your vagina? Or scraping a razor blade along the vaginal walls? Now that's a nasty thought!

Those who know the V words aren't interchangeable and still refuse to call a vulva a vulva, I charge with trying to desexualise a woman's sexiest parts. One of the things a vulva encompasses, that a vagina does not, is a clitoris, and a clitoris is that unique thing—a body part with no purpose whatsoever other than to give its owner sexual pleasure. The vulva also includes the labia, which swell and darken when their many nerve endings are stimulated. To call a woman's entire genital area a vagina ignores these sources of sexual pleasure and display, and assumes that her sexual function is as a receptacle for the male sexual organ.

The most egregious abuse of this language comes, unsurprisingly, from the people who are guilty of physically abusing women's genitals—the cosmetic surgeons specialising in 'vaginal rejuvenation', which is what they call the practice of slicing, dicing and stitching a woman's most sensitive bits. No one seems to be keeping figures on how common this extreme surgery is, but the surgeons are quick to tell us that everybody's doing it. An Australian 'vaginal' surgeon told a cosmetic surgery conference that he used to see only 'the professionals—the pole dancers, the strippers' but now he was seeing a lot of 'young girls who are concerned that their partners in sex may in fact be put off by the appearance of their vulvas'.

There are a number of surgical procedures that come under the heading of 'rejuvenation'. The Laser Vaginal Rejuvenation Institute of Los Angeles promotes its Designer Laser Vaginoplasty as the 'the aesthetic surgical enhancement of the vulvar structures, labia majora, mons pubis, perineum, introitus and hymen'. Note the word 'aesthetic' there. This is not surgery to correct an abnormality or to fix a functional problem. This is surgery to make a woman's genitals pretty. Pretty according to whom, you may well wonder.

'Many people have asked us for an example of the aesthetically pleasing vulva,' say the good doctors Simopoulos and Matlock (men, both) of the LVRI. 'We went to our patients for the answer and they said the playmates of *Playboy*.'

And what does it take to get a *Playboy*-perfect pussy? First, you'll need the Laser Reduction Labioplasty to trim your labia minora so that 'the small inner lips [do not]...project beyond the large outer lips'. Next, you'll want to have that laser applied to the 'excess skin along the sides of the clitoris', so as to provide a 'true playboy aesthetic look'.

Now that all that icky excess skin (otherwise known as delightful erectile tissue filled with nerve endings) is taken care of, it's time for your Augmentation Labioplasty which will give you 'aesthetically enhanced and youthful labia majora by...removal of fat via liposculpturing and transplanting it into the labia majora'. Bye bye chunky thighs, hello plump labia majora.

But wait! Isn't fat a bad thing? Why yes it is! That's why the LVRI offers Vulvar Lipoplasty to 'remove unwanted fat of the mons pubis and upper parts of the labia majora...to alleviate the unsightly fatty bulges of this area and produce an aesthetically pleasing contour'.

Now that you have a *Playboy*-pretty front bottom, it's time to clean up the back bottom with a Laser Perineoplasty to 'rejuvenate the relaxed or aging perineum'. And because even a girlishly pretty pudenda and perineum can be womanly on the inside, the compassionate medicos offer Hymenoplasty which 'can repair the hymen as if nothing ever occurred'. So you won't only look like a little girl, your dream man can feel as though he's penetrating one too!

The cosmetic surgeons point to porn mags as the source of

women's angst about the appearance of what the Manhattan Center for Vaginal Surgery calls—with the precise terminology one would expect from medical professionals—'the outer vagina'. Certainly, as we'll find, porn users can develop unrealistic expectations about the female body. But I think there's something more going on here, something caused by, or at least exacerbated by, our culture's coyness if not outright distaste for women's genitals.

It's true that mainstream porn champions the hairless, girlish genital aesthetic. But, as Helen Vnuk's *Snatched: Sex and Censorship in Australia* points out, so too does the Australian Office of Film and Literature Classification (OFLC). The OFLC guidelines for unrestricted publications (meaning they can be displayed in a newsagency without a sealed cover) say that 'realistic depictions may contain discreet genital detail but there should be no genital emphasis'. 'Genital detail' means protruding labia and so 'only exists in the context of female nudity'. If a publisher wants unrestricted classification it must ensure that any vulvas depicted are, as the graphic designers at girly mags the *Picture* and *People* put it, 'healed to single crease'. Despite its echoes of injury and medical intervention the phrase refers to the practice of digitally air-brushing photos before publication to remove visible labial tissue.

The result is that the pictures in both soft-porn and women's magazines are necessarily unreal. *Cosmopolitan*, for example, was not allowed to run unaltered photos in an article about, yes, the photoshopping of vulvas. As Vnuk points out, women in our society don't tend to partake of communal bathing, nor do they have the whip-it-out toilet habits of men; and so the only time straight women ever see the genitals of other women is in porn or women's magazines. For women to get a realistic view of female genitals, hard-core porn wins out over the ridiculously censored off-the-rack mags. At least the hard-core stuff sometimes shows that women have something other than a desexualised 'single crease'.

The obsession with Brazilian waxing seems to come from a similar desire to desexualise women's sexual organs. The waxed clean look is sometimes 'tidied up' even further by body make-up to cover pimples and redness, as well as anal bleaching to complete the fresh-off-the-production-line dolly look. You know how Barbie has a smooth, tan curve where her genitals should be? That's the look that's totally in right now: doll-like sexlessness. I reckon the reason poor Britney got so much flack for her flashing was that she failed to cover the caesarean scar, thus shattering the illusion of plasticised perfection her vulva promised.

As a result, young women are given the impression that there's something inherently wrong with their bodies. It's not just the refusal to call a vulva a vulva, or the jokes about fish smells and looseness, it's the fact that the only female genitals we are allowed to see have been tucked, cut, waxed and trimmed. Nobody knows what a real cunt looks like anymore.

See how much I love you?

A US *Details* magazine feature, 'Why Fat is Back in Hollywood', pointed to 'curvy' actresses like Drew Barrymore and Catherine Zeta-Jones to prove how sexy 'big' women are. (The article was accompanied by a photo of the back half of a pig wearing high heels. Charming.) A costume designer interviewed for the piece sounded exactly like the guys Lucia has been meeting: 'I'll tell you something—the chubby chicks aren't the ones turning the lights off during sex.' But none of the women mentioned in the article is anything like 'chubby'. These women are 'curvy', and curvy means large breasts, but without the upper arm, thigh and belly softness that often comes with them.

To meet the beauty ideal you must be stick thin and have large deposits of fat on your chest. Since this is all but impossible to achieve naturally, we have breast enlargement surgery, which is on the extreme rise. Over 250,000 American women had the surgery in 2004 which is a seven *hundred* percent increase since 1992. In Australia, the number of women having the surgery has 'at least doubled' in that same period, according to a *Good Weekend* interview with the former president of the Australian Society of Plastic Surgeons.

Thus, in men's magazine world, as in mainstream pornography, the ideal woman is one who has suffered for her body, as evidenced by her fake boobs and tiny waist. I'd argue that this is the ideal *because* it is all but impossible to look that way naturally. Isn't it the worst kind of fantasy, that a woman would spend time and money, suffer pain and jeopardise her health, in order to look like a male fantasy?

Cauterised genitals and bodies carved from deprivation, silicon and scalpels are signs of female perfection because they are measures of how much a woman is willing to do to please men. Will she go without food? Will she have the hair ripped off her vulva, her labial tissue removed? Will she pay to have her chest sliced open and have foreign objects inserted? Has she accepted—accepted so completely that it is literally written into her being—that her primary role is as an object of sexual pleasure for men?

Most women don't accept that, and most men don't expect us to. But what about those of us who see and reject the men's mag beauty standards, who would no more get a labioplasty than cut off our left arm, yet still feel like failures because we don't look the way we (illogically, ridiculously) think we should look?

It's all such a mess. I have admitted that, despite knowing how misogynous and false the beauty ideals of mainstream media are, I continue to hate my appearance. And, by the same sad logic, I have no expectation that anyone reading this chapter will be cured of body insecurity. This stuff goes deep. But there is one thing that made a small but significant difference to my thinking on this, and because I'm an optimist I have to think that relating it will somehow make a difference to the way other women think about their bodies.

When I was twenty-nine, the body I had always hated suddenly seemed to hate me back. I felt headachy, then dizzy, then paralysed with pain. I started vomiting and couldn't stop. My vision came and went with terrifying randomness. By the time the doctors found the clot blocking the blood flow on the right side of my brain, I was only intermittently conscious. I was admitted to the neurology ward and hooked up to machines and monitors and drips. As I slowly recovered, I began to think a great deal about my body: how it felt, what it could and couldn't do—and, why, when it had never given me any trouble at all, I had hated it all these years.

I considered my arms, for example: fleshy, pale, peppered with freckles and moles, the left one bearing the gruesome scar of a childhood accident. I'd kept them covered whenever possible, but during my illness they were the focal point of my care. My right arm was permanently attached to a drip containing the drug that was saving my life. My left arm was the site of three-hourly blood tests to check the levels of that life-saving drug. The fat blue veins on my inner arm were bled thin and pale by day three. Veins too tiny to see—on the inside of my wrists and the back of my hand—had to be clamped and drained instead.

My arms were not what I thought they were. There was not, in fact, nearly enough flesh to protect me from the constant handling and my skin was, within days, no longer pale but mottled with purple fingerprint bruises and red-black needle marks. My childhood scar became a streak of pretty pale pink against the new, darker colours.

It wasn't just how they looked; my arms were not my own to control. While chatting to a friend I gestured in my usual way and an arc of blood spurted out, spraying us both. When my husband visited I couldn't hug him, couldn't reach for him. I realised how lonely, how disconnected, how unlike myself I felt when I was, as I had always thought I wanted to be, effectively bodiless.

In hospital, contemplating my body piece-by-piece, I realised that it was a marvellous self-repairing machine, that the parts I hated the most for their appearance could perform life-saving functions, and, most of all, that it constantly provided me comfort, pleasure and the means to connect with those I loved.

I wish I could say that my illness totally and permanently changed the way I felt about myself, but eighteen months on, I can only say I'm getting there. I still hate the way I look, but I waste less time worrying about it than I used to. And on the days when all my personal baggage mixes with the cultural noise and makes me feel my lack of beauty is the single most important thing about me, I focus on the pinprick scars on my arms and remind myself that a body does not exist to be looked at (although looking can be very nice) but to work and move and touch. It helps. A little.

8
Pornstars and the Women Who Love Them

Discovering shame, discovering self

I first watched a porn film on a late summer afternoon just before my fifteenth birthday. A friend and I had skipped school to get drunk at the house of an older boy whose parents were away for the week. We were maybe a third into a shared bottle of Cinzano when a naked woman, bent double and peering between her own legs, appeared on the widescreen TV. The boys in the room became louder, perhaps to be heard over the moaning (fed through state-of-the-art stereo speakers), or perhaps out of the same edgy embarrassment that made my friend and I giggle. Everybody pretended not to care about what was happening on the screen—we drank and shouted and smoked even as we each kept the action on screen in our peripheral vision.

By the time the video ended (meaning a dozen podgy, hairy men had ejaculated on or in several young, busty, alarmingly vocal women) I felt deeply ashamed. Not because I was wagging school to get drunk with a bunch of older kids I barely knew, and not because everything I was doing that day (that year, even) would make my parents weep. I was ashamed that, up until now, I had been going around thinking I looked all right. I was ashamed because at least one of the boys in the room had seen parts of my body that I now knew were completely unacceptable.

That sense of shame (which it has taken me a good fifteen years to banish) is a significant strand in the tangled web of my feelings about pornography. Another strand is the research, by the Office of Film and Literature Classification, along with a 2007 report, *Understanding Pornography in Australia*, indicating that a third of porn users are women. Most users (of both sexes) say it has had a 'positive effect' on their lives. The shame I felt as a teenager contradicts the experiences of women who report that porn reduces or eliminates shame because it opens up sexual possibilities and shatters sexual taboos.

I am a woman of strong opinions and yet on the topic of pornography I am on the fence. And this is a spiky, uncomfortable fence for a feminist to be on, because this issue feels so important. I feel that any time I make concessions towards porn I am dooming a generation of young women to that sense of shame that has haunted me; and that any time I condemn porn I am condemning the thousands of women who have found sexual joy through pornography. This confusion may make me a wishy-washy feminist but it also puts me in a good position to examine the so-called porn wars—the battle over whether pornography helps, harms, or does nothing except waste bandwidth and time.

Mainstream misogyny

Anna Brownfield is a Melbourne-based university lecturer and self-described 'feminist erotic filmmaker'. I figured that since she's spent a decade thinking on and addressing the subject of feminism and porn she'd be a good guide, and I was right. I met her in a hip café where she talked passionately and unselfconsciously about her relationship to and experience of pornography and the porn industry. (The café was empty of customers but at one point I worried that the waiter may overhear our conversation and take offence. Anna laughed and told me that he had acted in one of her films and so was unlikely to be shocked by anything he heard us say.)

Anna makes films featuring hard-core, explicit sex but she prefers the term 'new-wave erotica' to pornography. 'As soon as you say the word porn,' she tells me, 'there's a certain assumption about how it looks, what it contains, how people will react to it sexually and so forth, so we really wanted to move away from that.'

She finds mainstream porn 'extremely boring…it's so formulaic, it's so orientated towards a male point of view…I just find it dull.' Worse than dullness, though, is 'the violence and debasement that is part of mainstream porn,' Anna says. 'I find it really objectionable.'

A note about the word 'mainstream' when applied to pornography: given that porn depicts actual rather than simulated acts, I'll say that what it is illegal to *do* (forced sex, sex with children or animals) is also illegal to *watch* in any language. There's no shortage of such material both online and off, but such things are so obviously harmful and destructive both to the victims being filmed and society as a whole that they don't bear discussion in the context of this book. Mainstream means the stuff you can buy or rent in a Main Street store or the stuff you can download without fear of the Feds bursting your door down and seizing your computer.

To get an idea of what mainstream porn contains these days I visited Australia's biggest online porn emporium *AdultShop.com.au*. Amongst the 'recommended' DVDs on the site was one in which the lead actor 'tours the former Soviet empire, defiling the sweetest young Russian girls with his enormous cock', another which boasts 'over 7 incredible hours of huge cocks in tight asses...double anal penetrations, gaping anuses...the hardest action', and an absolute charmer that promises you'll 'see lashings of milky sperm splatter on the faces, in the asses and down the throats of beautiful models'. The descriptions made me think of American journalist and anti-porn activist Robert Jensen's description of pornography as something which tells 'men stories about sex in which women are three holes and two hands, not people'.

If that sounds harsh it should. Mainstream pornography is overwhelmingly misogynous, not only because of its content (as if that weren't enough) but because of how it is made. When you watch scenes like those promised in the DVD blurbs above, you're not watching actors pretending to be double penetrated; those women are really experiencing that pain. If there's a 'gaping anus' on screen then there's one in real life, too. And if you let yourself wonder why the hell 'the sweetest young Russian girls' or anyone else would volunteer to do this stuff, you'll be led to the uncomfortable conclusion that they don't always volunteer. The women you see in porn are sometimes there because they are desperate for money or because they've been forced, drugged, tricked or coerced. (It's impossible to find reliable figures, but the anecdotal evidence suggests I might get away with 'often' rather than 'sometimes' here. You won't find anyone on either side of the argument who claims 'never' is the appropriate word.)

Luke Ford, a journalist and former porn actor who made a name for himself with his online porn gossip column, told the American 'Sixty Minutes' program that 'most girls who enter this industry do one video and quit. The experience is so painful, horrifying, embarrassing, humiliating for them that they never do it again'. Porn actor and director Brandon Iron, who specialises in 'group facials', a genre in which multiple men ejaculate on to a woman's face at once, told an Adult DVD magazine that when he asked some actresses to 'lick clean' a woman who had just been ejaculated on, 'some girls [did what was asked] with gusto, but others had to have their heads forcibly moved into position and ordered to start licking!'

Even Jenna Jameson, arguably the most famous porn actress in the world and someone to whom pro-porn types point as an example of how women in porn are powerful and in control, comes across as deeply damaged in her autobiography *How to Make Love Like a Porn Star*. She reports being gang-raped at a young age and then being exploited by various men throughout her early career. She also writes of her own drug addiction and the deaths and downfalls of other drug addicts in the industry. One of the most telling (and heartbreaking) incidents she recounts is when she applied for her first job as a stripper.

So desperate was she for money that she removed her own braces with a pair of pliers because they made her look too young to strip.

Bad enough that many porn users are getting off—unknowingly or unthinkingly—to women who have suffered humiliation, rape and coercion, but when you realise that there are whole brands and genres explicitly promising their audience that the women involved were tricked or abused it's hard not to be horrified. The popular soft-core *Girls Gone Wild* franchise consists of short documentary-style films of young women in bars and nightclubs taking off their clothes in exchange for a GGW trucker cap or T-shirt.

Guys Gone Wild (also produced by Mantra, the maker of *Girls Gone Wild*) is nowhere near as popular as the female-focused original. Re-gendering the series was never going to work, because going wild is what boys are expected to do, particularly when they're on spring break or out on the town with their buddies. Girls are supposed to be good and calm and sweet, and therefore their 'wildness' is not only a spectacle but it is probably something that has had to be encouraged by litres of beer and fast-talking. It's exciting to the audience because it's deviant, not because the women are actually 'wild'.

As part of his 1994 report on pornography, Robert Jensen watched and analysed three mainstream porn videos. 'At some point' in each video, according to Jensen, the actresses each:

> clearly appeared to a viewer to be in pain. Their facial expressions and voices conveyed that what was being done to them was causing physical discomfort and/or fear and/or distress. Given the ease with which video can be edited, why did the producers not edit out those expressions? There are two possible answers. One, they may view these kinds of expressions of pain by the women as of no

> consequence to the viewers' interest, and hence of no consequence to the goal of maximizing sales; women's pain is neutral. The second possibility is that the producers have reason to believe that viewers like the expressions of pain; women's pain helps sales.

Once you start looking at mainstream porn across all genres and formats it becomes obvious that although the specific actions of the performers vary (though not by an awful lot) the *frisson* often comes from the sense that the women either do not like or do not understand what they are doing. In the extreme, this takes the form of rape porn, but the idea that the woman had to be tricked or coaxed into performing for the cameras is a strong narrative strand in many less extreme genres.

Two popular series in the 'girl-on-girl' category, *Girls Hunting Girls* and *We Live Together*, for example, follow the same storyline: two actresses 'hunt down a girl on the street' and then 'talk her into' having sex on camera. These films don't show nearly as much explicit sex as those of other genres; the bulk of their running time is dedicated to showing a 'mall slut' or 'trashy hitchhiker' being cajoled into removing her clothes, then kissing another woman, and then having sex. The sex is almost beside the point. The thrill is in wearing a woman down until she's doing what she said or implied she wouldn't.

Even the soft-core stuff sold in newsagents infantilises the woman and emphasises her innocence. She may not have been tricked or forced, but she is so darn sweet and naive that there is the sense of the man having corrupted her. Think of *Playboy*, surely as mainstream as porn gets, and the girls with fluffy bunny ears and short cutesy bios about how they love skiing or baking. They are soft and unthreatening;

the fantasy is to bend them to your will, to sully their sweet, blushing, cheerleader innocence.

Playboy is, of course, a Disney cartoon compared to most of the stuff produced for internet or DVD in the last decade. Anna Brownfield, who keeps track of such things out of professional interest, told me that 'porn is getting more and more extreme'. Anal sex, for example, is now a standard porn 'move' and although this is not necessarily a brutal practice, the way it's performed in porn usually is. A bit of spit on the woman's orifice is all the preparation and care the men take. Then there's the choking: in porn, fellatio is the act of having a penis shoved down your throat until you can't breathe.

As for humiliation, Brownfield reports that porn isn't porn these days unless it ends with the man ejaculating on the woman's face, an act that, while not inherently humiliating (between two people who trust each other and agree on certain kinks, for example), is almost always presented as humiliating in the context of porn. The woman may have started the scene looking intimidatingly hot, but at the end she is prone, her make-up smudged, her hair sticky and her eyes watering (the always delightful Brandon Iron says that 'some women' have told him that semen in the eyes feels like 'battery acid'; naturally, he insists she must still act as though 'she craves it'). In the end she is nothing more than a place for the man to unload.

When Brownfield was trying to raise capital for her latest film she approached a big player in Australia's online pornography industry with a funding proposal. The man, 'who will remain nameless', told Anna she was mad for bothering with arty, female-friendly porn. 'He told me that everyone wants more and more hard-core and asked why he would put money into an Australian film when he can go to some

Eastern Bloc country and get some girl to do double penetration?'

Jensen quotes porn director Mitchell Spinelli making a similar comment: '"People want more. They want to know how many dicks you can shove up an ass," he says with a shrug. "It's like Fear Factor meets Jackass. Make it more hard, make it more nasty, make it more relentless."'

According to industry types, this is all consumer-driven, which makes me wonder who is spending money to watch women suffer in this way and how does it affect them, the viewers?

My friends Helen and Alison—both gorgeous, confident, professional thirty-year-olds—share a porn collection and swap the DVDs back and forth. 'There's always been this idea that women are not visually stimulated, and I think that's rubbish,' says Alison. 'That's always annoyed me. You know, "Women don't watch porn and women who do watch porn are horrible skanks." It's ridiculous. Men say, "Oh, women are just motivated by emotion." It's like "please!"'

'It really does make you go to town,' says Helen, who only watches porn 'with a boyfriend'. 'It's definitely an aphrodisiac...But the second you're done it's the most revolting thing.'

Helen's comment is indicative of many women's complicated relationship with pornography. Brownfield tells me about 'a nice lady in her sixties...who said "It's all exciting when you're watching it, but once you come it's just horrible!"'

When I ask Helen and Alison how they feel about the women in the movies they watch, there is a long silence. 'I don't judge them,' Alison says.

But does she think about how they feel?

'Sometimes you see this flash of boredom in their eyes and that sort of clicks you in to reality,' says Helen. 'That's a real person, there.'

I ask another friend, Dave, how he feels about the women who perform in his extensive collection of porn DVDs. 'I don't feel anything about them. I get off watching them, then I turn the film off and don't give it another thought.'

Isn't that awfully cold?

He rolls his eyes. 'What about other actresses?' he asks me. 'Do you think about the feelings of the people you watch in non-porn films?'

Well, okay, no, I don't often think about how non-porn actors and actresses feel when they are making their films. But sometimes I do. I haven't been able to watch *The Accused* since I read that Jodie Foster cried so hard she burst a tear duct during the filming of the gang-rape. The pain she suffered playing that role distracts me from the story in exactly the same way that knowing about the pain suffered by some porn actresses stops me from becoming aroused while watching porn. But, even so, there is a difference here. Foster was extremely well compensated in terms of pay and respect (she received the industry's highest honour, the Academy Award, for the role). So, yes, there is a difference between mainstream acting and porn acting, and yes it is possible to be concerned about the well-being of the performers in both cases.

So, Dave and plenty of other men remain respectful, moral and loving with wives, girlfriends, female colleagues and daughters, even though they happily admit to enjoying the occasional session of *Girls Gone Wild* or *Bangbus 3*. But even though porn does not turn all men into misogynous beasts, this is not a particularly comforting fact.

These men may be able to see women as fully human and worthy of respect, but they differentiate between 'real' women and porn women. Thus, some women (mum, wife, daughter, boss) are equal to men and worthy of all the same rights and respect, but women who have sex or remove their clothing for money belong to a different species. This species looks like a woman and sweats and breathes and sometimes even talks like a woman, but she is other, less than, and can morally and justifiably be treated as such. I've heard men justify their porn-watching by arguing that 'it's just a fantasy—I wouldn't treat a woman like that in real life'. But someone *did* treat a woman like that in real life to create the image. That stuff really happened; that's the point.

Women viewers of mainstream porn do something very similar. They see themselves as better than the women they are watching, as of a different class. There is a sense of power, too, involved in being able to pay someone to perform for your satisfaction, and women are not immune. Often, women who tolerate their partner's porn without enjoying it themselves become particularly hateful towards the performers. I think there is more to this than simple jealousy. If they've seen the men in their lives turn into either lust-filled morons or vicious pigs when confronted with such women, they may turn their disgust towards the object of his lust and/or scorn. The woman becomes the villain, the evil whore who has turned a good guy bad.

Playboy Bunnies in Wednesday Addams' clothes

The internet has revolutionised pornography, not only by providing access to an endless amount of porn featuring an endless variety of sexual activities, but by altering the social context of its consumption. In times past, you needed to purchase porn from a retailer. Whether hard-core from a sex-shop, soft-core from the local Blockbuster, or a titty-mag at the newsagent, there was a gatekeeper of sorts between the porn and the user. Now porn is unprecedentedly private and unrestricted. No one has to know about your lactation fetish. No one needs to know you are only fourteen years old.

The internet is also the site of a new front in the porn wars: the alt-porn battle. Alt-porn (as a huge, multi-million-dollar category, rather than a private homemade kink) is an internet-based phenomenon. It's like regular porn except the women, and occasionally men, are styled in ways that suggest they belong to alternative sub-cultures. The Playboy Bunny is replaced by that weird girl with pink hair, tattoos and facial piercings, and the background is some grungy bar rather than a satin-swathed boudoir, but it's still mostly naked women cupping their breasts and spreading their legs.

The largest and best known alt-porn site is *SuicideGirls.com* which describes itself as 'a vibrant, sex-positive community…founded on the belief that creativity, personality and intelligence are not incompatible with sexy, compelling entertainment'. One of its founders 'Missy Suicide' says she wanted to 'celebrate the diverse and beautiful real world women' by creating 'an alternative to the mainstream media's obsession with the silicone-enhanced Barbie dolls and the incredible shrinking starlets'. It was started in Portland, Oregon in 2001 by Missy and a bloke who calls himself 'Spooky Suicide', and now claims over five million visitors every month.

The site is all pink and black retro-chic with flashing banners urging you to sign up for US$4 a month and to purchase SG products, including T-shirts, underwear and books. (SG is more than a porn site, its press page claims: it's a 'contemporary lifestyle brand'.) The name is disturbing: the grim 'suicide' coupled with the infantilising 'girls'; but despite the name and the young emo models, the site has an upbeat, hip feel to it. The message board conversations are like a naughty slumber party, all dirty jokes, sincere affection and the odd drunken-sounding dramatic declaration.

The photo sets are mostly unremarkable. Women—often in costume or uniform—strip, frame by frame, until they are naked. There's an occasional leg spread or simulated masturbation, but it's all very tame (by online porn standards). What is striking is that the women look like humans rather than inflatable dolls, and they mostly look like they want to be doing what they're doing. There's not a milky-eyed, drugged-out stare in the lot of them.

I think the site might have comforted me at fifteen. There are small breasts, saggy breasts, uneven breasts, and, yes, more than a couple of pairs of fake breasts. Some models have bad skin or crooked teeth. Some have a touch of cellulite or a tiny roll of fat around their middles. Some are so thin you can see their ribs through their back. All of them have admirers who post comments about how desirable they are.

The models also have online journals. In some cases these are little more than Playboy-style blurbs about the girl's favourite animal and her desire for world peace. But many of the models do appear to be engaged with the site and its members, writing about their jobs, what they've been reading, their families or their love lives. Unlike the carefully managed images of models in mainstream porn, *SuicideGirls.com* does seem to allow its models to express themselves as three-dimensional human beings. 'Nexus', a twenty-one-year-old art student from Iowa, writes about how tough she's finding college and work and says she thinks she is suffering from depression. 'A lot of days I feel worthless,' she writes. The accompanying photo set shows Nexus wearing Hollywood-red lipstick, stockings and long black gloves. I find it hard to appreciate her lithe, pale-skinned body because her eyes seem filled with the melancholy she describes in her journal.

It worries me to think of people getting off over naked pictures of a messed-up girl like Nexus. But, on the other hand, it's got to be a positive that men who might otherwise see her as nothing but tits and spread legs may read her journal and acknowledge her humanity. Or am I being too optimistic about the sensitivities of internet-aided masturbators?

I don't think so. The message boards and member profiles give lie to the idea that all porn consumers are dirty old men or pimply-faced teenagers. When twenty-two-year-old Australian *SuicideGirl* 'Seven' writes about her miscarriage, members post their condolences and one man tells of his own baby's premature birth.

The alt-porn I looked at might have spared the teenage me from a feeling of shame about my non-pornified body, but the genre nevertheless does push its own version of the 'perfect woman': tattoos, dyed hair (blue-black, magenta or peroxide), piercings and pale skin. And even if the women look 'alternative' (or, you know, *normal*), the existence of the site is still dependent on the idea that women must look a certain way for the pleasure of a male audience. Just because you're all done up like Bettie Page doesn't mean you're retro or transgressive. It's only another costume like air hostess or naughty schoolgirl. And just because there's a list of your favourite books beside your naked pictures, you can't kid yourself that the customers would keep on paying if you decided to leave your clothes on while you talked literature.

In a sense, sites like *SuicideGirl* are more troubling than mainstream sites because they let the buyers off the hook. A man can pretend to himself that he is deep, sensitive and caring because the chick he's wanking over is, like him, deep and sensitive, not like the big-titted blond whores at *hotwetsluts.com*. The *SuicideGirl* models fit the perfect image of a certain type of guy who loves girls who are tortured and angsty, who write poetry and maybe cut on their wrists a little, who are wild and crazy angry and tough, but who are also small and vulnerable and in need of a deep, emo dude to help them cope with life. And also, they're way sexy. The men who get off on this particular male fantasy get to masturbate to images that make them feel like a saviour rather than an exploiter.

Objects speak

It is often argued by pro-porn feminists that pornography can help women explore their sexuality by helping them discover what turns them on and by helping them communicate their discoveries to partners. 'A lot of women do find it hard to communicate exactly what they like,' says Anna Brownfield. 'I think a lot of women use pornography as a tool to say to their partner, "Ooh, this kind of looks exciting. Let's try that."'

But there's a flip side to using porn as a tool of female empowerment. Mainstream porn demands its female performers meet the same beauty standards as fashion models. The more upscale brands might insist on catwalk-model beauty, while the lower-class gonzo-style films accept a K-Mart catalogue aesthetic, but it's still all about being thin, young and pretty. Body hair—except for the occasional 'racing stripe' over the pubic mound—is completely unacceptable. As mentioned, alt-porn is slightly less prescriptive about bodily perfection and depilation, but it's still about how much the appearance of your body turns the customers on.

As for the educational aspect, this too can be more problem than solution. Anna notes that 'a lot of young men or boys get their sexual education from pornography, like there's a lot more anal sex going on, it's becoming expected'. It's something that my buddies Alison and Helen have noticed out on the singles circuit too.

'Porn moves are all well and good in the confines of a relationship,' Helen says. 'But when it's a one-night stand and the guy starts pulling these bullshit moves…they've obviously watched a lot of porn. They have this really horrible idea of what sex should be with women. It's sort of a violent, tacky…' She puts her hands up as if to stop the thought.

Alison takes over. 'The things they do and you go "porn watcher!" There are just a couple of signature porn moves. Like they hit your nipples or try and hit your clitoris or something…They can be really rough.'

Helen and Alison are old enough and have enough experience to be able to vocalise their displeasure when a sex partner starts acting all XXX Cowboy on them. But what of younger women whose same-age partners have grown up with hard-core pornography just a mouse click away?

Laura is twenty and has been involved sexually with three men of about her own age since she was seventeen. All three were unapologetic porn users. Two of them commented on her abundance of pubic hair, saying they were used to seeing women with smooth pubises. One of them attempted to have anal sex with her the first time they slept together. The other two waited 'less than a month before trying it'. All three men acted 'offended and confused' when she batted them away. 'I don't know whether guys think it's enjoyable for women or they don't care, but they totally expect it.'

If young people look at pornography as a way to learn about the opposite sex and about sex as an act, they also look to it for instructions on their own sex—how a person should look and behave in order to arouse another person. As most porn is produced by men for a male audience, the lessons girls are learning about their sexual role is from an overwhelmingly male point of view.

Just as I, at fourteen, felt covered in shame at my own physical imperfection when I watched porn, many women I spoke to reported feeling not only aesthetically wrong but sexually inept. 'I can't give head properly,' confessed one twenty-four-year-old. What did she mean by 'properly'? 'Like, I can't get it in all the way and I have to stop after a while. I've tried to keep going but my whole face starts to hurt.'

Other women I spoke to made similar comments: for every sex act and position there was a woman who told me she was sure she wasn't doing it correctly. When I asked what they meant, they described some extreme super-human performance. When I asked where they got the idea that this was 'proper' they invariably said 'porn', 'the movies' or 'my boyfriend says'. When women responded with the last I asked if said boyfriend was a porn consumer; without fail the women said yes and in every case they made it clear that I was naive for even asking the question.

But not all young women respond to pornography with thoughts of worthlessness or sexual incompetence. Some of them watch porn and decide that some men will judge women no matter what they do.

Laura saw her first pornographic magazine when she was twelve. It was being pored over by her older brother and his friends and they let her 'read' it with them. 'I pretended I was totally cool about it,' she says now. 'But I felt really awful. It wasn't so much that I was shocked by the pictures—I wasn't completely innocent and the mag was pretty tame. I was upset at the way they were all laughing at the girls in the pictures. It seemed so mean to be laughing at them when they were trying so hard to look sexy.'

Karin had a similar experience on viewing her first porn video, at the age of fourteen. 'I was turned on, which was a bit weird since I was at a party and everyone else seemed to think it was just a joke. One of the things everyone was laughing at was how ugly the woman looked when the guy's dick was in her mouth. It was like, no matter how hot you are...no matter if you do this thing guys say they love, you just end up an ugly slut.'

And, as nasty a message as this is, its reception may be a positive thing. After all, a woman who understands that acting like a pornstar isn't going to win her love, respect or even mild affection will more likely follow her own bliss rather than that of a porn-trained partner.

A new wave

In all this discussion, it's important to emphasise that there is nothing inherently degrading about people having sex on film. The vast majority of porn is misogynous and degrading to women because it is reflecting dominant cultural values. Similarly, the abuse of women within the adult film industry is only to be expected when our culture for the most part treats women as inferior, especially overtly sexual women. Stigmatising porn may only make the problem worse, as it encourages people to see women who perform in porn as automatically degraded. It's not inconceivable that this attitude would spread outside of porn to perpetuate further the idea that any woman who enjoys sex is degraded.

And although most porn is shockingly inaccurate in its depiction of sex, it's worth noting that romance novels, TV soaps and many Hollywood films are equally guilty of fostering unrealistic expectations of love and sex. But while it is true that many other media products treat women like objects and perpetuate sexism, this is no reason to let porn off the feminist-critique hook. If, as feminists, we are going to call out the fashion industry on its portrayal of women as pretty dollies who exist to be dressed up, then we must also call out the pornography industry on its portrayal of women as pretty bodies that exist only to be fucked.

Brownfield points out that because of the 'taboo associated with viewing pornography…people don't question what they're seeing, or think they don't have a voice in what they're seeing'. Men and women who enjoy porn but hate its misogyny need to take this to heart. They need to stop giving pornography a pass simply because they're too embarrassed to critique it in public or because they think that there *should* be something 'wrong' about porn. There is absolutely nothing wrong with consenting adults getting off by watching other consenting adults getting off; what's wrong is the misogyny. It's the people who buy and enjoy porn who can fix this if they demand a quality, non-sexist product.

Writer, academic and porn researcher Kath Albury provides a checklist for ethical porn consumption:

- Does the web page or video suggest that sexually active women are stupid or naive?
- Does it imply that it's OK to trick or manipulate women into acts they don't want to perform, because, after all, they're 'just dumb sluts'?
- Does the plot-line or image suggest a disregard for the performer's health and safety?
- Does it place performers at clear risk of sexually transmissible infections? Are condoms used? Does the company that produces the pornography subscribe to the guidelines of the Adult Industry Medical Health Care Foundation (*www.aim-med.org*)?
- If consumers are not sure of the answers to these questions, they should ask for more information. If that is not forthcoming, they should exercise their rights to seek out explicit material that meets their ethical standards.

Brownfield's film, *The Band* (Hungry Films, 2007), meets all of Albury's criteria. The women are active, knowing participants, often taking the lead and requesting certain acts. Condoms are visible in every penetration scene, and gloves and lube are used in an anal play sequence. There are no surgically enhanced breasts or genitals, and the male and female actors are a variety of sizes and shapes.

The Band stands out from mainstream porn I've seen, too, because the camera spends as much—possibly more—time lingering on the male bodies as on the female. As men masturbate, penetrate and are themselves penetrated, we get lengthy, close-up shots of their penises, legs, hands and faces. The plot, though minimal, adds context to the sexual acts. Male and female characters have names, jobs and personalities which do not dissolve or become indistinguishable from each other during sex.

The Band was still in post-production and had not yet been through the censor at the time of writing, but there are plenty of other ethical, erotic films out there if you know where to look. A good starting point is the website of Toronto sex shop Good For Her (*goodforher.com*). Here you'll find the recipients of its Feminist Porn Awards, which 'recognise and celebrate the good porn makers'. Winners are judged on several criteria including that 'the film expands the range of sexual expression for women'. Among the 2006 contingent is director Tristan Taormino whose aim is 'to create images that contradict (and hopefully challenge) other porn that represents women only as objects and vehicles for male pleasure'. Also check out *NoFauxxx.com* (which 'strives to break down all sex stereotypes and typecasting, providing an in-depth analysis of the porn industry while creating hot porn') and *forthegirls.com* ('sex-positive, feminist...hot porn site and hip online webzine').

The availability of porn that is not misogynous will only increase if the market for it increases. So rather than secretly consume porn that degrades women, speak up about your desires and be as discerning about what you're buying as you would be about any other media product.

9
Boy Trouble

Nervous wrecks, metrosexuals and nerds

In some circles (ultra-conservative religious ones usually) feminism is the enemy of all that is good and wholesome in the world. It is also the enemy of men. Feminists, if you listen to this lot, are all man-hating lesbians (or sometimes man-hating sluts) who want to abort male foetuses or raise boys to be slaves to a cold, heartless matriarchal regime. Within this regime women will lord it over their personal empires of boy-slaves and chained-up emasculated men. Families, miniskirts, home cooking and perky cheerleaders will be distant memories.

To anyone who believes even a skerrick of the above, I say time to don that tinfoil hat and hunker down waiting for the end of days.

To those who don't believe that feminists are evil but *do* maintain that we have weakened the dominance of the nuclear family as society's foundational unit, I say not yet but we're trying. If you want to give feminism the credit, go right ahead. You can also blame us for the criminalisation of marital rape and the end of forced adoption of babies born out of wedlock, if you like.

Then there are those who feel that it's all right for the chicks, but when the big pink powder puff of feminism comes near men it turns them all soft and gooey. Or as former leader of the Australian Labor Party Mark Latham put it, that 'mates and good blokes' are transformed into 'nervous wrecks, metrosexuals and nerds'. His words amusingly echo those of Boy Scouts of America founder Ernest Thompson Seton, who, as sociologist Michael Kimmel points out, was worried over a century ago that boys were turning into 'a lot of flat-chested cigarette smokers with shaky nerves and doubtful vitality'.

These haters and worrywarts aside, there are a large number of reasonable, women-loving men—some of them progressive liberals, even—who shun feminism because they think it is irrelevant now that women can vote and buy property. These fellas have no problem treating the women and girls in their lives with respect but they don't get why feminists go on about how tough it is to be a female while ignoring the plight of men.

When Melbourne writer Sushi Das published an opinion piece in the *Age* asking why men did not engage in feminist debate, she received 'a tsunami of email'. In a follow-up piece, she wrote that in the majority of emails 'anger appeared to be the underlying emotion because the writers believed the pendulum had swung too far in favour of women'. The men were angry, because they apparently felt 'women's needs took priority over theirs...men constituted the majority of the unemployed, the homeless, the victims of industrial accidents and suicides...men's health received less funding than women's, and boys' education was poor'.

As Das wrote, 'These are real concerns, but how many can really be blamed on feminism?' Her answer, and mine, is *none of them*.

I like to think of men who are angry at women as being feminists who've not yet seen the light. The gender-specific woes of men are, like the gender-specific woes of women, caused by a crazy system of inequality. The men complaining about how tough men and boys have it would do well to join the feminist cause.

Biological determinism and why feminists are men's biggest defenders

It's weird to blame anti-men sentiments on feminism. The idea that men are useless/cruel/uncontrollable sex beasts/any other negative generalisation is, in fact, profoundly un-feminist because it is based on a biological determinism which is the antithesis of feminist thinking. If we say all men are [whatever], then we're saying they can't help it, boys will be boys, snails and puppy-dog tails, etc. Feminism is about acknowledging that adults of either sex are responsible for their own actions. It's a position that judges individuals for their behaviour, not their gender.

Accepting that men are inherently violent is a small step away from accepting that men cannot help being physically abusive, that assault, rape and murder are somehow natural behaviours for them. And accepting that women are inherently passive is a small step away from telling girls that they are not expected to stand up for themselves, that there is something wrong with a girl who fights back.

These stereotypes are not only dangerous; they are wrong. According to psychologist James Garbarino, girls and boys are equally aggressive for the first three years of life, after which girls are socialised to swap 'assertive physicality' for verbal interaction. So, by their teenage years, girls generally have better skills for coping with conflict without resorting to physical violence. Accordingly, women's preference for the verbal over the physical is learned behaviour, no more 'natural' than a preference for skirts over jeans.

To be clear: feminism never says that men and women are exactly the same. But the vast majority of gender differences are socialised, not natural, and are not significant enough to justify unequal legal and social treatment of women. A common misconception about feminism is that it means taking something—power, rights, status—away from men. But feminism is about restoring the rights, power and status of women so that they match those of men; no taking, no giving, simply restoring the natural order. And it *is* the natural order unless you believe that men are inherently more deserving than women.

Women still have much work to do in overturning or at least adjusting their cultural roles. Feminism has both been part of and necessitated this process; the feminist movement has always been populated by women interested in opening up our culture's definition of 'woman'. This radical (but unfinished) work of expanding the meaning of femaleness has not, unfortunately, been matched by a corresponding men's movement. The men's movements that have sprung up in response to feminism's challenges are overwhelmingly those whose members yearn to crush feminism and return women to the home.

There are a few exceptions. Michael Kimmel's book *Manhood in America* is a history of the changing face of masculinity in American culture, and his edited anthology *The Politics of Manhood* collects pro-feminist men's thoughts on feminism and its opponents. Michael Flood, another leader in this field, is Postdoctoral Fellow at the Australian Research Centre in Sex, Health and Society (ARCSHS) at La Trobe University. He says that 'the idea that feminism is anti-male' is a 'pernicious lie' and that, in fact, 'it makes perfect sense for men to support feminism'. His work as a coordinator of pro-feminist, male-focused website *XYonline.net* and of the male-driven anti-domestic-violence campaign, White Ribbon Day, is based on the 'fundamental belief that the relations between women and men can be democratic and pleasurable'.

The dilemma at the heart of male reactions to feminism is rooted in the fact that the traditional values of masculinity depend on the oppression or subservience of women for their expression. Man as protector and breadwinner. Man as warrior. Man as leader of his family/workplace/people. When women can and do protect, feed, fight and lead for themselves, many men feel redundant. But that's life in the patriarchy: we feel bad if we can't play the roles we've been trained to play.

The solution is far more complex than I'm going to make it sound. But here goes, anyway: first, men need to take leadership in broadening the definitions of masculinity. This is already happening to some extent with men like Michael Flood, Michael Kimmel and others who write and critique traditional masculinity and look for alternatives.

Important to the male-initiated breakdown of gender norms, too, are the men who are not activists or polemicists or politicians, but who simply live their non-sexist masculinity every day. Two such men are Les and Ben Pobjie (otherwise known as my dad and my brother). My dad, a shearer's son, grew up in a country town, left school at fifteen, and built a career in newspapers out of grit and determination. My brother, a newspaperman's son, grew up in the suburbs, has a tertiary education, a passion for writing and performing comedy and a night job that allows him to support his wife and baby boy. These are not politically or socially radical men, but they are, nevertheless, examples of the way individuals can quietly revolutionise what it means to be a man in our society.

Here's an excerpt of Ben's blog entry to celebrate his first Father's Day:

> For most of my life I have been a sporting fanatic. But I have never felt at ease with sporting culture. I've played sport, I've loved sport, I've liked a lot of the people I've played sport with, but the drinking, the vulgarity, the sexism, that goes hand-in-hand with sport, never liked it. And never felt pressured to be a part of it. Just enjoyed the game. And that's because that's how my father is...I've never felt I have to get into stuff I don't want to in order to be more of a man...Because that's how my father is. My father does what is right, he doesn't buy into myths or stereotypes, but nobody is more of a man than my father...

It's important that men work at redefining masculinity, whether through activism or as living role models. But to have a society where neither gender is demonised or oppressed, we also need to work at annihilating the idea that men are one way and women another and that only one sex can be on top. It is nonsense to say that if women can protect their families men are not needed, and it also denigrates the value of partnership. It's possible—preferable even—to have a partnership in which both adults are capable and willing to feed, protect and defend the family. A woman who can take care of herself is in a relationship willingly, not out of necessity, and thus that relationship—that *family*—is likely to be stronger.

A family in which a man is only needed to keep the wolves from the door is, of course, going to fall apart if the woman learns how to do that job for herself. But if the man is there because he and his wife love and support each other and want to build a future together, then there is nothing threatening about the woman being able to fight off metaphorical wolves. They can take turns or do it together or hire a professional wolf-fighter to take care of that while they both go to work. At night, they can both light a fire and huddle together and shiver at the idea that either should have to face wolves and jobs and life alone.

Trouble with boys

The 'trouble with boys' has become a favourite media trend story, with commentators, politicians and various experts positing that girls are enjoying unprecedented academic success at the expense of boys.

In the US, boys are 50 percent more likely to repeat a grade in elementary school, one-third more likely to drop out of high school, and about six times more likely to be diagnosed with attention deficit and hyperactivity disorder than girls. In Australia, boys in Years 3 and 4 trail girls of the same age by around 4 percent when it comes to meeting the national literacy benchmark. By the time kids are fifteen, the gap has widened, with 69 percent of fifteen-year-old Australian girls scoring at or above the OECD mean in reading literacy tests, compared with 55.4 percent of males, according to a 2003 government paper, 'Educating Boys'. In the UK, a 2007 paper from the Higher Education Policy Institute in Oxford found that 40 percent of girls take A-level exams (the main route to university entry) as opposed to only 30 percent of boys, but the results of boys and girls are much the same.

Michael Kimmel points out that, although the percentage of female admissions to colleges in the US has increased from 38 percent of girls in 1960 to 70 percent today, so too has the percentage of males going to college risen from 54 percent to 64 percent. Yes, the rate of increase is higher for women but the fact remains that the percentage of Americans going to college has increased overall. Kimmel further notes that the top universities in the US including Harvard, Yale, Princeton, Berkeley and MIT enrol more men than women. Only Stanford has a roughly equal gender balance.

In the UK, in 2006, the UCAS (Universities and Colleges Admissions Service) recorded fewer than 45 percent of male university applicants. Australia had a similar percentage (45.9) of male applicants in 1992, but ten years later that had dropped to 43 percent. An extensive research project into boys' education, commissioned by the Commonwealth Department of Education, Science and Training (DEST), concluded that while:

> there are indeed problems for some boys in terms of their engagement and involvement in schooling…this report emphasises the need to go beyond viewing boys as a homogenous group. The

> research also found that good teaching...impacts significantly on positive learning experiences for both boys and girls.

Most significantly, the report concluded that 'it is simplistic to reduce the issues involved with boys' education to an understanding of boys as being essentially different from girls in their approach to learning'.

So to talk about girls' success as being responsible for boys' (perceived) lack of success is to set up a false dichotomy. To talk about girls thriving at the expense of boys assumes that their needs are mutually exclusive, as though we must choose to educate and raise girls *or* boys, but not both.

Professor Johanna Wyn, director of the Youth Research Centre at Melbourne University, told the *Age* that the concerns of boys and girls are very similar, although 'the way they carry their concerns is different'. In other words, while the specific desires and needs may vary (although very often they don't), the things boys need from the education system—authority figures, parents and society—are the same as the things girls need—guidance, acceptance, encouragement, love and occasional discipline. The core precept of feminism, to treat every individual as an individual, would seem the best foundation for encouraging kids of both sexes to develop into confident, responsible adults.

Nevertheless, there are many who insist boys are suffering because girls are advantaged by the very structure of modern schooling. Seventeen-year-old Boston high school senior Doug Anglin made headlines around the world in 2006 when he filed a federal civil rights complaint against his school on the grounds of sex discrimination. Anglin contended that the school's grading and discipline policies favoured behaviour which came naturally to girls while punishing the rebellious ways of boys. 'From the elementary level, they establish a philosophy that if you sit down, follow orders, and listen to what they say, you'll do well and get good grades. Men naturally rebel against this,' according to Anglin.

His is the only case I know of where legal action has been taken against a school, but it generated a flood of commentary and books, which have over the last five years, rehearsed the argument that classrooms are too feminised and boyish behaviour has been pathologised.

'Beginning in very early grades, the sit-still, read-your-book, raise-your-hand-quietly, don't-learn-by-doing-but-by-taking-notes classroom is a worse fit for more boys than it is for most girls,' wrote Michael Gurian in the *Washington Post* on 4 December 2005. It's an argument that is often repeated, but it's got nothing to do with feminism at all. When have classrooms been tolerant of rambunctious, 'boyish' behaviour? When was this golden age of education when boys were encouraged to run through the hallways yelling and get up from their desks whenever they felt like it? In what era did boys not have to read books and write essays and say please and thank you? Oh, and can somebody please tell me when girls became compliant, obedient little angels who love sitting still and concentrating and who never, ever talk out of turn, run inside or shout across rooms?

Gurian references Huck Finn to support his thesis that boys can't sit still; I see his Huck Finn and raise him Jane Eyre: 'Women are supposed to be very calm generally; but women feel just as men feel; they need exercise for their faculties and a field for their efforts as much as their brothers do; they suffer from too rigid a restraint, too absolute a stagnation, precisely as men would suffer.'

Nonetheless, there is a molehill of statistical (and a mountain of anecdotal) evidence suggesting that boys are having a tough time at school, particularly reading and writing. Many who refer to a 'feminised' education system, or classrooms 'protective of the female learning style', assume that subjects relying on 'female' verbal skills and empathy disadvantage boys who are naturally crap at words and emotions. (Nobody mentions Shakespeare and Milton and Keats and all those other wordy, emotional fellas.)

For those who doubt that teens are influenced by their peers beyond the areas of fashion and music downloads, the DEST research makes interesting reading. The researchers found 'there were significant differences between the genders in peer group influences, with some boys indicating that they were subject to more negative peer pressures and were more likely to adopt anti-school attitudes and more limited subject choices'. The report also noted that 'homophobic put-downs were often used to insult those boys who were identified as not conforming to dominant and stereotyped ways of being male, including in some schools those boys with pro-academic attitudes'. Dr Peter Cox of La Trobe University reported similar findings to the *Age* in 2006. His research showed that studious boys felt they had to be 'covert' about their study, or risk being labelled 'uncool' or 'gay'.

What a loop we're stuck in: these subjects are perceived as being feminine, thus boys either don't bother trying or they downplay their natural ability, and the whole thing starts over with educators and pundits fretting that boys aren't doing well in these girly subjects. Exactly the same pattern occurred with girls and maths/science subjects back before big bad feminism. The solution was to de-stigmatise the subjects girls were avoiding, not to change the curriculum to suit girls' imagined inherent inability to think in a linear fashion.

'Patriarchy is the single most life-threatening social disease assaulting the male body and spirit in our nation.' bell hooks

If the worst consequence of gender stereotypes for boys was a slightly lower tertiary entrance score there'd be cause for concern but not alarm. But alarm seems an under-reaction when you understand that the same system of compulsory masculinity that tells boys they'll be fags if they top English is also damaging them emotionally, psychologically and physically.

When I say 'system of compulsory masculinity' I'm talking about what Michael Kimmel, in his essay 'A Black Woman Took My Job', calls 'the four basic rules of masculinity':

1 No Sissy Stuff. Masculinity is based on the relentless repudiation of the feminine.
2 Be a Big Wheel. Masculinity is measured by the size of your pay check, and marked by wealth, power and status.
3 Be a Sturdy Oak. What makes a man a man is that he is reliable in a crisis. And what makes him reliable in a crisis is that he resembles an inanimate object. A rock, a pillar, a tree.
4 Give 'em Hell. Exude an aura of daring and aggression. Take risks; live life on the edge.

If we then look at the problems that affect teenage boys, and later men, we see much evidence for these beliefs. Teenage boys are more likely than teenage girls to be involved in a car crash, commit violence against others (of both genders), have problems with the law and abuse alcohol and drugs. All of these behaviours fit with rule 4 and some of them could also be associated with the 'No Sissy Stuff' rule. Boys are also more likely to commit suicide than girls, something that could be related to all of the above rules working together, but, most particularly, rule 3: a boy in suicidal distress may appear as troubled as a rock and be dead before anyone watching could hope to help.

Research by the Johns Hopkins Children's Center shows that holding 'traditional beliefs about what it means to be a "real man"' can undermine the sexual health and good preventive care of teenage boys. 'Stereotypes about masculinity suggest that for boys, seeking care is a sign of weakness, and our analysis shows that such beliefs can be considered a health risk factor in and of itself,' according to the report's author, Dr Arik Marcell.

Past the especially high-risk teen years, males are still at risk and sexism is still to blame. Most workplace injuries and deaths happen to men. According to the US Department of Labor, in 2005, men were 54 percent of the workforce but constituted 93 percent of fatalities at work. This is not surprising when most dangerous jobs—mining, construction, driving—are dominated by males. Likewise, 2004 US Bureau of Labor statistics reveal that 94 percent of workplace suicides are men. Again, not surprising when the jobs with the highest suicide rates—police, farmer, military—are male-dominated fields.

There are a lot of reasons men are the ones doing the dangerous work but they can all be brought back to two beliefs: that men are tougher and stronger than women, and that men's lives are worth less than women's. That's it—every excuse society gives for placing so many men in danger (and so many more when we're at war) comes down to these two beliefs. Men can hack it. Better a dead man than a dead woman.

The same arguments come up when talking about the role of women in war. On 7 April 2007 in response to a news story about the rape of female soldiers in Iraq, Kathleen Parker wrote in the *Washington Post:* 'What kind of man, one shudders to wonder, is willing to allow his country's women to be raped and tortured by men of enemy nations? None that I know, but our military is gradually weaning men of their intuitive inclination to protect women—which, by extrapolation, means ignoring the screams of women being assaulted.'

It's okay to send young men off to torture and be tortured, to kill and be killed, but sending women to the same fate is wrong? The screams of women should inspire more horror than the screams of men? This sickens me. I don't mind saying that my husband is the most precious person in my life. I'm appalled that anyone would treat his life as cheaper than mine because he happens to be male. Likewise, my nephews are as precious to me as my nieces. I can't fathom a worldview that says otherwise. How exactly does placing value on a person according to their gender show respect for women or men as individuals?

It seems paradoxical that, in a society in which men dominate the halls of power, men are generally considered expendable. It makes more sense when you realise that the men in power are no more representative of men in general than they are representative of women in general. The men treated as cannon fodder and paid killers in a time of war are not the men in power. The men who work each day in poorly paid, back-breaking jobs with shocking safety records are not the ones in power.

Feminism does not treat men as stupid, worthless, uncontrollable, savage, dangerous or expendable. The system that does that is called patriarchy and we live under one. It's a system that relies on restrictive gender roles as a means of keeping us all under control. If the men stay in their place and the women in theirs, and if when they do meet they are filled with misunderstanding and bitterness and resentment, then maybe they will never recognise each other as friends and allies; and they will never join together to make things better for all of us.

Men keep doing the dangerous work and getting sick and suffering and dying because they think they'd be lesser men if they didn't. Women watch the men and boys they love suffering and taking risks and dying early and they feel helpless because they believe that is just the way men are. And meanwhile women are suffering in all the ways I've described and the men are helpless because they think that women just are like this: body-obsessed and fickle and tired and self-hating. We become immune to the depressed boys and abused women, to the seething men and the desperate women.

That's how the patriarchy works. We think it's normal. We think it's just the way men are, women are, crazy world, can't live with 'em, can't live without 'em. Except we're all living without each other, really, aren't we? We're all responding to a bunch of stereotypes and perceptions and costumes.

In 2006 Joss Whedon, creator of cult TV shows 'Buffy the Vampire Slayer' and 'Firefly', was honoured by the human rights organisation Equality Now for his 'outstanding contribution to equality in film and television'. In his acceptance speech he talked about his frustration at being asked 'again and again and again' why he writes such strong female characters. After repeating some of his typical answers ('because of my mother'; 'because of my father'; 'because they're hot') he let fly with his real answer:

> Because—equality is not a concept. It's not something we should be striving for. It's a necessity. Equality is like gravity. We need it to stand on this earth as men and women. And the misogyny that is in every culture is not a true part of the human condition. It is life out of balance, and that imbalance is sucking something out of the soul of every man and woman who is confronted with it.

10
Why Sexual Freedom Is So Scary (and So Important)

First they came for the homosexuals...

While a culture is of course affected by its political context, most of the gender roles we inhabit are rooted so deeply that simply voting for one party over another, or changing isolated policies, has minimal impact. In some cases, however, the reverse is true: sometimes, the political is personal. A particular party or leader, for example, will set an agenda or pass a law that has an impact on the private lives of individuals. The individuals thus affected are not, then, responding to cultural pressures, but political or legal edicts.

There's a widespread belief that in secular democracies—like Australia, the UK and the US—sex discrimination is illegal and that every adult has the same political, financial and legal rights. This is simply not true. Plenty of people in our so-called equal society have lesser rights, by law, because of their gender or sexual orientation. I'm talking mostly about gay, lesbian and transgender people, but also about certain categories of straight women—the underage, the poor, the uneducated and the abused. In recent years, there has been a frightening number of attempts, some of them successful, to minimise the rights of these people even further.

Australia is the land of mateship and the fair go, except when it comes to same-sex relationships. In 2006, the Treasurer, Peter Costello, affirmed that, with regard to gay people in Australia, 'we do not criminalise conduct or behaviour'. Those lucky gays—falling in love and having consensual sex without being carted off to jail!

Same-sex attracted people in Australia have second-class rights. In 2004, the government passed the Marriage Legislation Amendment Act which enshrines the definition of marriage as 'a union of a man and woman to the exclusion of all others', thus pre-empting any state legislature's approval of same-sex marriages. When the Australian Capital Territory (ACT) passed civil union legislation giving gay couples the same rights as married couples, the federal Attorney-General Philip Ruddock promptly overturned the law. In June 2007, the Human Rights and Equal Opportunity Commission (HREOC) released a report, called 'Same-Sex: Same Entitlements', demonstrating that Australian gay couples 'face systematic discrimination on a daily basis' including in the areas of superannuation, taxation, social security, workplace entitlements and health care.

The laws in the US, as in Australia, vary from state to state, but, unlike Australia, some US states recognise that same-sex couples are entitled to equal rights. By November 2007, same-sex marriage was legal (but under challenge) in Massachusetts, and civil unions were recognised in California, Connecticut, Hawaii, Maine, New Jersey, Vermont, Washington, and the US District of Columbia. What exactly 'civil union' means varies from state to state, but it usually includes legal recognition of the relationship for tax and healthcare purposes.

Katrina Fox, self-described 'slightly kinky high-femme, high-camp lipstick lesbian' is the editor of *Cherrie*, a Sydney-based monthly fashion, entertainment and pop culture magazine for urban lesbian/queer girls. She also writes news, features and a weekly column, Keeping Abreast, for *SX* magazine, a publication for the gay, lesbian, bisexual and transgender (GLBT) community in Sydney. It's her private rather than professional life, however, that I want to speak about because her experiences demonstrate the absurdity of legislating relationships according to the gender of the participants.

Katrina's partner of thirteen years is a fifty-year-old British woman who had gender reassignment surgery at twenty-two. Until very recently British transsexuals could have their gender changed on their passport but not on their birth certificate. In 1997, Katrina and her girlfriend became frustrated that as a same-sex couple they had no legal recognition (British law has recognised same-sex couples only since 2005). They decided to take advantage of the fact that one of them had a male birth certificate and to marry as a heterosexual couple. 'It caused a bit of a kerfuffle,' Katrina tells me, 'as the man at the registry office didn't believe she was born male and we went to the press to make a point, but we got married, completely legally, in England.'

Then the story gets really outrageous: 'We moved to Australia in 2001. I was granted my temporary visa on the basis of being my partner's legal spouse. However, when we applied for permanent residency, the Australian government turned around and said it would not recognise our legal British marriage because it would mean we were two women married!'

So the UK recognises Katrina and her partner as a legally married 'heterosexual' couple while Australia says they are a same-sex couple and as such have none of the rights or benefits bestowed upon married couples.

'Neither of us is interested in marriage for its own sake,' says Katrina, 'but at the moment, we don't have the benefits of straight, married couples...I think it's most unfair that they recognised our marriage initially and let me into the country because of it, but then changed their minds when I applied for a different visa, purely because of their institutionalised homophobia.'

Sam and Kelly Pilgrim-Byrne are another Australian couple who've battled the bureaucracy in order to have their fourteen-year relationship legally recognised. Like Katrina and her partner, the Pilgrim-Byrnes were not interested in marriage for marriage's sake, but, after the rigmarole of having to prove to various bureaucracies that they were a legitimate couple, they had to concede 'that it would be far easier to just be able to marry and be recognised as a couple immediately'.

'De facto couples...are being penalised for not joining the "institution of marriage",' the Pilgrim-Byrnes say. 'Problem is, same-sex couples in Australia can't join it, even if only for practical reasons like us.'

The name-change was important to Kelly and Sam, because they wanted to be recognised as a family when their baby came along. Their experience of fertility treatment is something to which many straight couples will relate, but, as in so many other areas of life, there are additional barriers and stresses for same-sex couples like the Pilgrim-Byrnes.

In August 2006, the HREOC held an inquiry into discrimination against same-sex couples in Australia, and the Pilgrim-Byrnes decided to make a submission to the Western Australian public hearing. The bulk of their submission concerned their struggle to conceive:

> Three years after starting treatment, we estimate we have spent at least $30,000. We have re-financed the home once, and will likely have to do so again...Often we sit in the waiting room of our fertility clinic and look around us at the many other couples struggling with infertility. What isn't lost on us, however, is that we pay more for our treatment than they do and that their struggle is legitimised by the Government with financial support that we don't receive.
>
> In addition to this, we are unable to relieve some of the financial hardship by taking advantage of federal legislation in other areas—such as taxation and superannuation contribution splitting...We pay twice into a system that provides no recognition of our long-term commitment to one another and we can't for the life of us understand why this is so. How this is fair.
>
> We are continually asked why we don't just adopt. The truth is, we would do so in a heartbeat, except that the countries that have an agreement with Australia will not adopt to gays or lesbians.

As I was working on this chapter, a heartbreaking story appeared in the *Sydney Morning Herald* and drove home the injustice of legal discrimination against same-sex couples. Jiro Takamisawa nursed his partner of twenty years, a World War II veteran, through the final years of heart disease. Takamisawa qualified for a widow's pension according to the application form, which does not ask for the applicant's gender. Nevertheless, his application was rejected, as were his appeals to the Veterans' Review Board, the Minister for Veterans' Affairs and the Attorney-General. The HREOC declined to investigate and so, as a last resort, Takamisawa will take his case to the United Nations Human Rights Council. If justice serves, the UNHRC will recognise that if Takamisawa were female he would receive the pension and, as such, this is a clear-cut case of gender discrimination against an old man who has lost the person he loved and took care of for so many years.

Then they came for me...

Pregnancy is the great divider in every human society. Throughout history, women have been forced into subservience because the extra nutritional needs and the lessened ability to work meant they often relied on the benevolence of men to keep them fed and protected throughout pregnancy. Throughout history, women have also developed and attempted means of contraception and abortion in order to reduce their dependence on never-pregnant men.

And now we have the scientific and medical knowledge that allows us to prevent or delay pregnancy. We also have, in the first world, such fabulous things as maternity hospitals and supermarkets and professional cleaners, which mean that a pregnant woman or new mum can use her hard-earned cash to provide for and protect herself and her child, no manual labour or male benefactor required.

We've had this freedom for less than fifty years as compared with thousands in which women were slaves to their biology and therefore, in most cases, to men. Women's equality (such as it is) is very new. It's also very much under threat.

American sex advice columnist Dan Savage has been warning his readers for some time about 'the anti-straight-rights agenda' of the American government. It used to be that only far-right-wing religious types opposed women's reproductive rights, but no more. For the past several years, legislators across the US have been chipping away at the rights of women to control their own reproduction. Then, in November 2006, President Bush appointed Eric Keroack as a senior advisor for the federal program supervising birth control and family planning funding. Keroack's previous position was as medical director of A Woman's Concern, an anti-abortion, anti-contraception organisation. It would be hard to think of a more radical opponent to reproductive rights; it would be hard to think of a more mainstream position for him to hold.

One of the hot topics across US state legislatures at the time of writing is the availability of emergency contraception, known in the US as Plan B. The reason conservatives are opposed to the drug—which prevents pregnancy if taken within seventy-two hours of intercourse—was expressed by a Bush-government appointee to the Federal Drug Administration (FDA) advisory committee, who says that it would 'increase sexual promiscuity among teenagers'. The deputy commissioner for operations at the FDA goes even further, fretting that availability of Plan B would cause 'extreme promiscuous behaviours' and 'lead adolescents to form sex-based cults centred around the use of Plan B'.

These people are opposed to medication to prevent pregnancy because they fear young women will then feel free to have as much sex as they like. This same fear motivates their opposition to RU486, a prescription drug that successfully terminates pregnancy in 95 percent of cases when used within forty-nine days of a woman's last period. Its advantages over surgical abortion include not needing anaesthetic, no risk of perforation or damage to the cervix and efficacy at terminating pregnancy several weeks earlier than surgical abortion can be performed. The drug is legal in the UK, most of Europe and in Australia, where it is highly regulated and remains controversial.

The FDA is investigating a challenge to its regulation of RU486, while some Republicans are agitating to have the medication banned outright. The doctor who advises the FDA on reproductive-health drugs told the *New York Times* he was 'fully committed to promoting an understanding of human sexuality and procreation radically at odds with the prevailing views and practices of our contemporary culture'. In other words, he doesn't want women to have access to this drug because he doesn't like the idea of people having sex for fun rather than reproductive purposes.

Isolated quotes from opponents to contraception and abortion can leave the impression that these folks are the loony fringe. If only this were so. In almost every legislature in the US, laws restricting abortion are either being considered or have already been passed. In some states, women must watch sonograms of their foetus, endure a mandatory waiting period or, if they are teens, receive parental consent, before they can terminate their pregnancy. In North Dakota, legislators have all but declared teenage girls the property of their parents by passing a law requiring girls under eighteen to have permission from a parent or guardian before they are given any pre-natal care, whether they intend to continue the pregnancy or not.

It's possible we'll look back on these measures and consider them mild. It's possible what we're seeing now is the beginning of the end of women's rights to abortion in America. In April 2007, the Supreme Court of the United States upheld the Federal Partial Birth Abortion Ban Act. What this means is that doctors who perform late-term abortions using the technique commonly referred to as intact dilation and evacuation (D&E), will face two years jail *even if the procedure was performed to protect the woman's health*. D&E is a rare procedure that is usually performed only after some miscarriages, or when there is a serious defect in the foetus that was undetectable earlier in the pregnancy. D&E procedures can be traumatic because the mother has usually carried her baby for an extended time before discovering the pregnancy is unviable. Women who receive this procedure are often left devastated; but, without it, they could be left dead or severely harmed.

The frustrating, nonsensical aspect of this ban is that it will do nothing to prevent foetal deaths, because it only prohibits particular means of performing abortions, rather than circumstances or timing. So, women who would have, in the past, had their non-viable pregnancies terminated by D&E can still legally terminate the pregnancy but only if the foetus is first injected with lethal chemicals and/or dismembered *in utero* before extraction. Both procedures are far more dangerous for the woman than an intact D&E.

No foetuses saved, no abortions prevented—what's the point? Well, Supreme Court Justice Ruth Bader Ginsburg, who dissented, said the ruling 'cannot be understood as anything other than an effort to chip away at a right declared again and again by this court'. Ginsburg said the decision 'tolerates, indeed applauds, federal intervention to ban nationwide a procedure found necessary and proper in certain cases by the American College of Obstetricians and Gynaecologists'. She said, further, that the court's view of women 'reflects ancient notions about women's place in the family and under the Constitution ideas that have long since been discredited'.

Ginsburg is not overstating the case. Writing the decision for the majority, Justice Anthony Kennedy showed his essentialist views of women by his insistence that 'respect for human life finds an ultimate expression in the bond of love the mother has for her child'. The decision also found that 'the government has a legitimate and substantial interest in preserving and promoting foetal life'.

In 1990, the Court of Appeals for the District of Columbia, overruled a court order that Angela Carder undergo a caesarean against her will. In its decision, the appeal judges declared that 'a foetus cannot have rights...superior to those of a person who has already been born'. The decision came too late for Carder and her baby, who both died shortly after the forced surgery. As Lynn Paltrow, the director of National Advocates for Pregnant Women, pointed out in the *American Prospect* in April 2007, the recent Supreme Court ruling effectively asserts the right of the original court in the Calder case to 'justify court-ordered Caesarean sections in cases where physicians believe that a c-section will prove more beneficial to the foetus'.

In Australia the situation is not as dire, but there are murmurings. In 2005, Liberal backbencher Danna Vale, calling for a national inquiry into abortion, said that while she believed 'in a woman's right to choice', she worried that women don't understand the 'tragedy of post-abortion depression'. This sounds like she is concerned about women's well-being. If that's the case, she can rest easy: a sizeable body of research exists to show that depression is no more prevalent in women who have had abortions than in the general population. And perhaps one of the reasons there isn't endemic post-abortion depression is that every woman who requests an abortion in Australia receives counselling about her choices and their respective risks.

It is insulting to assume women 'don't understand' the potential consequences of something that they may have talked about in depth with counsellors and doctors, and with women who've had similar experiences. And it plays into the hands of those who would take choice away from women—people like the anti-abortion activists profiled in the *New York Times* on 21 January 2007, who use the threat of post-abortion depression as a tool to convince legislators and the American public that 'for women's sake, abortion should not be legal'.

A lot of the 'limiting abortion' rhetoric comes down to a belief that abortion is not so much a right as a privilege granted to certain women in certain circumstances. Naomi Wolf has called on pro-choicers 'to recognise that some abortions are less moral than others'. Wolf is not alone: there is a widespread assumption that a woman who faces an unplanned pregnancy has done something wrong and so should expect to face consequences.

The fact is that somewhere between 40 percent and 66 percent of Australian and New Zealand women who consider abortion were using contraception when they fell pregnant. Condoms break, and even when the pill is used perfectly it has a failure rate of 1 percent. Then there are the things that reduce the pill's effectiveness: vomiting, diarrhoea, use of antibiotics or other drugs. There are women, particularly in rural areas, who do not have access to contraceptives due to location, cost, or because they encounter doctors and pharmacists who refuse to prescribe them. Sometimes women are raped or in abusive relationships or lack a strong enough sense of themselves to argue for their right to take sexual health precautions.

And sometimes women, like men, are irresponsible and reckless. It happens. Wolf berates 'men and women who choose abortion because they were careless or in a hurry or didn't like the feel of latex'. But parenting is a tough job requiring loads of responsibility; should we punish irresponsible people by forcing them to take on such an important job? Even aside from this, and allowing that a resulting child could be adopted, it is monstrously punitive to insist that a woman carry an unwanted pregnancy to term merely because she did something someone else thinks was irresponsible, particularly when the male partner retains control of his body for the nine months after ill-considered sex.

Attitudes such as Wolf's reflect a belief that a woman must earn her abortion by meeting certain criteria of morality or reasonableness. So, if the condom broke and you had no access to emergency contraception, you deserve one. If you're sixteen and were pressured by your overbearing boyfriend to have unprotected sex and now you've realised the error of your ways and dumped him, you deserve one. If you're thirty and this is your third unwanted pregnancy and you couldn't get to the pharmacist to buy the morning after pill, well, too bad, you haven't earned your abortion.

Like the modesty movement, the anti-reproductive-rights crowd believe the sexuality of women is something to be controlled by external forces. It is inherently misogynous because the responsibility and punishment always fall to the woman even as she is treated as incapable of managing her own reproductive health. In this logic, it is the responsibility of women not to dress or act in a way that will lead men to have sex with them. If they fail in not stopping men (or worse *themselves*) from having sex, then they should be punished with an unwanted baby. Nothing puts a woman in her place like nine months of unwanted physical and emotional exhaustion.

This is more than an attack on women's sexuality; it's an attack on the right of women to participate in society on equal terms. If women are at the mercy of men's sexuality, being unable to enjoy guilt-free orgasm is the least of our worries. We cannot make decisions about whether we want children. We cannot control the timing of our pregnancies. Aside from the horror of having our bodies used as incubators against our will, the unpredictable, uncontrollable cycle of pregnancy and birth makes career planning and financial independence difficult if not impossible. A woman without the ultimate say over her own body is a woman without control over her life.

Protecting the patriarchs

After the federal Attorney-General blocked his civil union legislation, ACT Chief Minister Jon Stanhope told ABC radio that 'Mr Ruddock needs to be asked what is his real concern about the ACT legislation, what is his real concern about my commitment to remove discrimination and to show respect to same-sex relationships'.

It's an important question. Most of us have, to varying degrees, an interest in the private lives of our friends and family members and we all have opinions on whether our best friend's husband is good enough for her or whether our cousin's celibacy is just a phase. But why are governments so interested in people's sex lives and family structures? Not interested in a mild, gossipy curious way either. They're so concerned about our individual love affairs and family dynamics that they're actively attempting to legislate them. I have to ask: as long as we all pay our taxes and obey the law, why does the government care who's sleeping, adopting, reproducing or setting up home with whom?

And I think I've figured it out: it's about protecting the patriarchy. (I know, I know, but bear with me.) Let's start with reproductive rights. There are a couple of reasons patriarchs are interested in what women do with their own uteruses.

First, the straightforward, economic reason: women who perform 'traditional' female roles provide society with free labour. The housewife keeps the home clean, cooks the food and provides childcare for absolutely nothing. Women also traditionally have performed, for free, services for which the state or private citizens would otherwise have to pay: charitable fundraising, volunteer duty at churches, schools and nursing homes, the care and feeding of elderly relatives. If women have jobs and the incomes and decision-making powers that come with them, then the state would have to spend considerably more on childcare, education, elderly care and other essential social institutions.

Then there's the nation-building motivation. Danna Vale opposed the RU486 bill out of fear that Australia could become a Muslim nation within fifty years because 'we are aborting ourselves almost out of existence'. Her appalling racism was much commented on in the mainstream press. Less noted, however, was the equally appalling sexism implicit in what was, essentially, a call to enlist women's bodies in this revolting racial numbers-game.

When you hear politicians or pundits railing against abortion or contraception or sex education, you may or may not be hearing a religious, political or moral argument. What you will certainly be hearing is an argument that requires limiting women's opportunities. Without access to contraception and the right to terminate an unwanted pregnancy, we lose control of our own destinies, and we lose the ability to participate in society on equal terms with men. Reproductive freedom is fundamental to women's freedom, and women's freedom is fundamental to gender equality.

This is where the gay rights issue comes back in. Putting aside those who are outright bigots and therefore do not need a reason to hate and discriminate, we can see that the very idea of same-sex *anything* to do with the family threatens the female-nurturer, male-provider model of society. If two men can raise a child, then that means that nurturing, cake-baking and bum-wiping are not inherently female qualities! If two women can raise a child then that means that breadwinning and security-giving and the ability to discipline are not inherently male qualities!

Gay marriage is evidence that gender equality is not only possible, but that it doesn't kill sexual, romantic or familial love. Gay families demonstrate that parenting and domestic responsibilities need not be distributed according to gender. They prove that two adults can choose to share a life and build a family based on mutual love and desire, rather than on playing out traditional gender roles.

Conservatives are terrified by the thought of non-traditional families. They're terrified by the idea that people cannot be defined, classified and assigned life-long roles simply by virtue of their gender. They're terrified that we'll all realise that a marriage which conforms to traditional gender roles is a choice, not the default. They're terrified that if the general population realises gendered behaviour isn't compulsory, then we might start really thinking for ourselves about other things too.

11
'Women Are Morally Superior!'
'Things Could be Worse!' (And Other Things People Say to Shut Us Up)

'Things were easier in the old days'

It is sometimes argued that feminism has made life more stressful for women. This may be true. When women had little choice but to become full-time mothers and housewives, the stress of negotiating the minefield of career and motherhood was non-existent. Entrenched gender roles meant fewer couples fought over who would care for the kids, cook dinner and take care of the family finances.

There may be other ways in which the daily existence of some women was easier when society was more sexist, but I can't think of any. It doesn't matter anyway; freedom and equality are human rights, not lifestyle choices. Slaves are in the position of having someone else make all the decisions about their lives, but nobody claims this is a benefit. Children are economically supported and physically cared for, but what adult wants to return to the dependency and lack of freedom of childhood?

Imagine arguing that men would be better off if they were confined to the home, uneducated and sexually oppressed. Imagine arguing that men should be denied *for their own good* the right to go out alone at night, play contact sports or join the defence force. One can point out that these activities are, to varying degrees, dangerous, but to tell a man he is incapable of weighing up the risk and making his own decision is to treat him as a child or mentally incompetent.

The situation is no different for women. Anybody who argues women were 'better off' when they were unable to go to university, work, vote, run for political office, own property or have sex without fear of pregnancy clearly considers them to be an inferior species. Such an argument positions us as sweet children in need of patronage and protection, rather than adults with the ability to observe, assess and decide for ourselves.

'Feminism promised we could "have it all", and failed to deliver'

In 2002, journalist Virginia Haussegger, writing in the *Age*, blamed the fact she was almost forty and childless on feminism's claim that women could 'have it all'. 'While encouraging women in the '70s and '80s to reach for the sky,' she wrote, 'none of our purple-clad, feminist mothers thought to tell us the truth about the biological clock'.

In a follow-up article the following year, Haussegger again attributed the problems of working women to feminism:

> The fact that the workplace remains dreadfully family unfriendly; that many working mothers are guilt-stricken and expect to be discriminated against by employers when their dual roles conflict; that many young women erroneously think they can postpone having children well into the second decade of their busy careers; and that an increasing number of young, fertile women are choosing not to have children at all, leads to some big questions for feminism.

Haussegger's 2005 book, *Wonder Woman*, builds on her *Age* articles. The book gives voice to the distress and disappointment many women experience on finding themselves childless in their thirties and forties. It is a moving work and admirable for its determination to tell the stories of unhappily childless women. There's no disputing the pain experienced by the women Haussegger talks to. The problem is that, as in the *Age* articles, Haussegger perpetuates the myth that this is all somehow the fault of feminists who promised women could 'have it all'.

As Susan Faludi showed in her 1992 book *Backlash*, 'what has made women unhappy in the last decade is not their "equality", which they don't yet have, but the rising pressure to halt, and even reverse, women's quest for that equality. The "man shortage" and the "infertility epidemic" are not the price of liberation; in fact, they do not even exist'. Furthermore, 'having it all', as Natasha Campo argues in the

Journal of Australian Studies in 2005, was never a feminist promise. It is 'a long-standing cliché used to dismiss women's achievements and desires', and 'a way of dismissing it as a movement that held out promises that could never be kept'.

In response to Haussegger's claims, writer, academic and literary critic Kerryn Goldsworthy published on her blog the finest defence of her generation's feminist legacy that I have come across. Describing herself as 'one of the traitorous feminists [Haussegger] blames for the fact that she has no children', Goldsworthy writes that:

> the very notion of being 'betrayed by feminism' is kind of bizarre. Those who live by any ideological framework and personalise it enough to be able to feel 'betrayed' by it when it doesn't meet their expectations were playing a mug's game in the first place.
>
> My own take on this question is the exact opposite: feminism has helped me make my way through what has not, at this time and in this place, been a particularly typical woman's life. It's shown me that I had choices, shown me what they were, predicted (rightly) what the difficulties would be, given me a framework for understanding and dealing with those difficulties, and given me a vocabulary in which to think and talk about them.

'Women are better than men'

At the turn of last century, Australian suffragists argued for female voting rights by claiming that women were, in some ways, better than men. They argued that women were 'uniquely qualified' in certain areas of society such as education, caring for the sick, and family life, and that these qualifications could be used in a way that would benefit not just individual households but the state. They also argued that women's moral superiority would help keep public life free of vice and corruption.

What's extraordinary is that the same arguments are still made today: that women have a civilising influence on society; that if women ran the world there would be no war; that we need more women in public life because women are empathetic, co-operative, good communicators, effective facilitators and on and on.

As was the case with the suffragists, it's likely some people making these arguments believe these things about women, while others believe that harnessing society's existing perceptions of women for the cause is easier than changing those perceptions. But, unlike the suffragists, we can today be in no doubt that the abilities of people are not determined by gender. Unlike the suffragists, we have the legal right to vote and run for political office. Unlike the suffragists, we have the legal right to earn money, own property and make decisions for ourselves and our families. Unlike the suffragists, we have no excuse for peddling stereotypes about women that are not only wrong but that actually damage the cause of gender equity.

Women, because of all those cultural forces discussed throughout this book, may indeed bring different ideas and qualities to political or workplace discussions from men. Knowing that if we have children we will need to make enormous and difficult decisions about our careers, for example, tends to make women more knowledgeable and thoughtful on issues of parental leave and childcare. But the more that men are expected to take equal responsibility for parenting, the more we will find them bringing that same awareness to the table.

Every time someone attempts to champion the rights of women by claiming women are superior to men, the gender divide is deepened. Each 'women are more empathetic' or 'all men are bastards' pits us against each other. Such comments—sometimes unthinking, throw-away lines; sometimes seriously intended—reinforce the cultural myth that men and women are fundamentally different not only biologically, but intellectually and morally.

At the same time, the qualities that supposedly make women better are reinforced as female norms, meaning that women who don't conform are labelled as unwomanly, odd or defective. And since it's impossible always to be kind, empathetic, nurturing, communicative, intuitive, unselfish and morally scrupulous we can *all* end up feeling, at some time, unwomanly, odd and defective.

'But men and women are *different. Look around!'*

Women and men have more in common than at any other time in history, and yet so many elements of our society still operate as though humanity is comprised of two separate species, each with its own biologically determined role to play. The differences *within* each gender are evidently greater and more important in terms of strengths, weaknesses, abilities and desires than those found between the two gender groups. Yet the myth that women are *this* and men *that* persists.

Evidence that people of both genders act in all kinds of ways is continually ignored in favour of reinforcing examples of people who conform to gendered expectations. The woman who melts at the sight of a baby is said to be demonstrating behaviour typical to her sex, while the man who does the same is merely a sweet guy. The man who shies away from commitment is being a typical bloke; a woman who does the same must be damaged in some way.

These may seem trivial examples—who cares if people expect you to love babies?—but they illustrate a pattern of thought that has serious implications. Consider two executives: one male, one female. Each has developed a reputation for leaving the office early to attend to his or her children. Each is considered a slacker by his or her workmates. However, because the female executive is conforming to a stereotype that says mothers make distracted, uncommitted employees, she is seen as representing her entire sex, while the male executive is derided as lazy, hen-pecked or, of course, acting like a woman. The woman's behaviour confirms a stereotype about women, and so does the man's.

'Western feminists should think about how much worse off women in third-world countries are'

Actually, that's true—feminists *should* educate themselves about the lives of women throughout the world. Here's a start: women make up 51 percent of the world's population but hold only 16 percent of parliamentary and congressional seats. They perform two-thirds of all labour and produce more than half of the world's food, yet own less than 1 percent of the world's land and property. Seventy percent of those living in poverty are female, as are two-thirds of all uneducated children and two-thirds of the world's illiterate adults. Eighty percent of the approximately 700,000 people trafficked into slavery (including sex slavery) each year are female. Thirty-three percent of women worldwide are victims of violence including rape and battery; in some countries this figure is as high as 70 percent. Every year, 500,000 women die during pregnancy and childbirth, 68,000 die and 5.3 million suffer temporary or permanent disability as a result of unsafe abortion. An estimated 130 million women and girls have been subjected to female genital mutilation, the consequences of which are increased susceptibility to HIV infection, childbirth complications and inflammatory and urinary tract diseases, and all these only if the girl does not first bleed to death.

If you are a middle-class woman living in a democratic country it is easy to forget that for many women in the world sexism and misogyny are daily and often deadly threats. You're probably so busy trying to juggle your own set of challenges that the misfortune of women half-a-world away doesn't register. Or if it does, it may reinforce what your culture tells you: that you have it pretty good and so shouldn't complain.

But women suffering serious human rights abuses are not helped, if we, who have it comparatively good, decide our rights are unimportant. What helps women all over the world is for each of us firstly to ensure we stay informed on these issues and never let the fact that women are global second-class citizens be forgotten.

One very important thing that women in Australia and the US can do is to be aware that our governments currently restrict foreign aid being spent on medical facilities or services which advise on or provide pregnancy termination. So in East Timor, for example, any clinic or facility offering advice on safe termination is ineligible for Australian or American aid dollars. This in a nation with an average birth rate of 8.5 per woman and a maternal death rate twenty times that of Australian women. Lobbying our own governments for change in policies that hurt women in other nations is something simple but significant we can all do.

The other very important thing we 'first-world' women can do to help those in less prosperous and less free countries is to ensure that women right where we live are treated like full human beings. If we drop the equality ball here at home we'll have neither the social and political clout, nor the moral authority, to change things elsewhere. If we each fight on our own frontline and send whatever intellectual, practical and financial resources we have to help our sisters and brothers in their battles, the position of women the world over is strengthened.

This, happily enough, means the well-being of people the world over is improved, because, as UNICEF puts it, 'gender equality produces a double dividend...healthy, educated, empowered women have healthy, educated and confident daughters and sons'. The double dividend is part of what senior fellow at the US Council on Foreign Relations, Isobel Coleman, is referring to when she writes that:

> significant research has demonstrated...[that] women are critical to economic development, active civil society, and good governance, especially in developing countries. Focusing on women is often the best way to reduce birth rates and child mortality; improve health, nutrition, and education; stem the spread of HIV/AIDS; build robust and self-sustaining community organizations; and encourage grassroots democracy.

'Feminists want to erase gender and make everybody the same'

Fighting for feminism at home means defending the belief that, while there are differences between men and women, none of them justifies one sex having more social, economic or political power than the other. Gender is not the problem; expecting half of the population to fit a particular gender stereotype, and rewarding or penalising individuals according to how successfully they meet those expectations, is the problem.

Destroying the 'slut' stereotype doesn't mean encouraging women to have more (or less) sex; it means refusing to judge women's sexual behaviour differently from men's. Questioning the 'princess' as role model, or the reasons women wear make-up, or the importance placed on female appearance, does not mean women should stop emphasising their femininity, but that such emphasis should be neither expected nor held up as an ideal against which all women are judged.

Feminism is about increasing options for women and men. It's about destroying the idea that there is a correct way of being female or male. There would still be princesses, pornstars, dedicated housewives and ambitious careerists if feminism succeeded in destroying gender-based inequality. But we could choose these roles. We each could choose to express, in whatever way we felt most authentic, our femininity, masculinity, androgyny, sexuality, asexuality, maternity, paternity, ambition, passion and any of the other complicated, endlessly variable elements that make up a human being.

Suggested Reading

Julia Baird, *Media Tarts*, Scribe, 2004

Simone de Beauvoir, *The Second Sex*, Vintage, 1952

Susan Brownmiller, *Femininity*, Ballantine Books, 1985

Leslie Cannold, *What, No Baby? Why Women Are Losing the Freedom to Mother and How They Can Get It Back*, Curtin Press, 2005

Angela Carter, *The Bloody Chamber*, Penguin, 1979

Kaz Cooke, *Girl Stuff: Your Full-on Guide to the Teen Years*, Penguin, 2007

Susan Faludi, *Backlash: The Undeclared War Against American Women*, Anchor, 1992

Betty Friedan, *The Feminine Mystique*, Penguin, 1963

Germaine Greer, *The Female Eunuch,* HarperCollins, 1970

bell hooks, *Feminism is for Everybody: Passionate Politics*, South End Press, 2000

bell hooks, *The Will to Change: Men, Masculinity, and Love*, Washington Square Press, 2005

Lisa Jervis and Andi Zeisler (eds), *BITCHfest: Ten Years of Cultural Criticism from the Pages of Bitch Magazine*, Farrar, Straus and Giroux, 2006

Michael Kimmel, *Manhood in America: A Cultural History*, Free Press, 1997

Ariel Levy, *Female Chauvinist Pigs: Women and the Rise of Raunch Culture*, Free Press, 2005

Susan Maushart, *Wifework: What Marriage Really Means for Women*, Text Publishing, 2001

Elaine Showalter, *A Literature of Their Own,* Princeton University Press, 1998

Anne Summers, *The End of Equality: Work, Babies and Women's Choices in 21st Century Australia*, Random House, 2003

Anne Summers, *Damned Whores and God's Police: The Colonisation of Women in Australia*, Penguin, 1975

Naomi Wolf, *The Beauty Myth: How Images of Beauty Are Used Against Women,* Vintage, 1991

Virginia Woolf, *A Room of One's Own*, Harcourt, 1929

Acknowledgments

This book would not have been possible without the assistance of a great many people.

Anna Brownfield, Michael Flood, Sarah Hunt, Sam and Kelly Pilgrim-Byrne, Katrina Fox and Annie Bennett were particularly generous with their time and knowledge.

Thanks also to Kath Albury, Kerryn Goldsworthy, Karen Willis, Donna Byrne, Ben Pobjie, Hilary Manning and Matt O'Dea for their contributions.

I am indebted to all of the women and men who shared their thoughts and experiences and allowed me to tell their stories in this book. I am especially grateful to those who did double duty as frontline informants and terrific friends: Rachel Palermo, Stephanie Hardy, Jo O'Dea, Alice Pobjie and Rebecca Davis.

Thanks also to Jeff Maguire, who makes everything better, and to Gaye and Les Pobjie and Gerry Maguire who all deserve more thanks than I can ever give.

Very special thanks to my editor Penny Hueston for her provocative questions, smart suggestions and unwavering enthusiasm.

Index